Scott Foresman

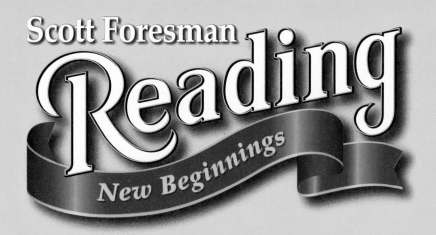

New Beginnings

You + Me = Special

Zoom In!

Side by Side

About the Cover Artist

Where John Sandford lives in Michigan, there are lots of small animals such as squirrels and chipmunks, but when he is painting an animal, he thinks about a person he knows. He says that thinking of a particular person as he works gives his animals personality.

John Sandford: cover

ISBN 0-328-03933-0

Scott Foresman Reading
New Beginnings

Program Authors

Peter Afflerbach

James Beers

Camille Blachowicz

Candy Dawson Boyd

Wendy Cheyney

Deborah Diffily

Dolores Gaunty-Porter

Connie Juel

Donald Leu

Jeanne Paratore

Sam Sebesta

Karen Kring Wixson

PEARSON

Scott Foresman

Editorial Offices: Glenview, Illinois • Parsippany, New Jersey • New York, New York
Sales Offices: Parsippany, New Jersey • Duluth, Georgia • Glenview, Illinois
Coppell, Texas • Ontario, California • Mesa, Arizona

Contents

You+Me = Special

Unit 1

5

Contents

Unit 2

Contents

Side by Side

Unit 3

You+Me =Special

What makes us all special?

Franny and Ginny

by Pat Cummings illustrated by Fred Willingham

Franny spied a ladybug
Sitting in the sun.
So her sister Ginny
Went and found another one.

12

"Franny, does your ladybug
Have three spots or two?"
Franny said to Ginny,
"Must you do just as I do?"

Franny got her pencils out.
She found some paper too.
Then she said to Ginny,
"Please, do not do just as I do."

Franny drew a flower.
Then Ginny drew one too.
So Franny said to Ginny,
"MUST you do just as I do?"

Ginny sprang up and left the room,
And Franny drew a strange green cow.
Then Franny had to wonder,
"Could Ginny need me now?"

Franny ran all through the house.
She found Ginny in her bed.
There she was, fast asleep,
With a picture by her head.

Ginny had made a picture
Of two sisters hand in hand.
As Franny saw what Ginny had done,
She now could understand.

Franny said to Ginny,
"I LOVE your picture. It is true."
Then she gave her sis a hug and said,
"I truly love YOU too."

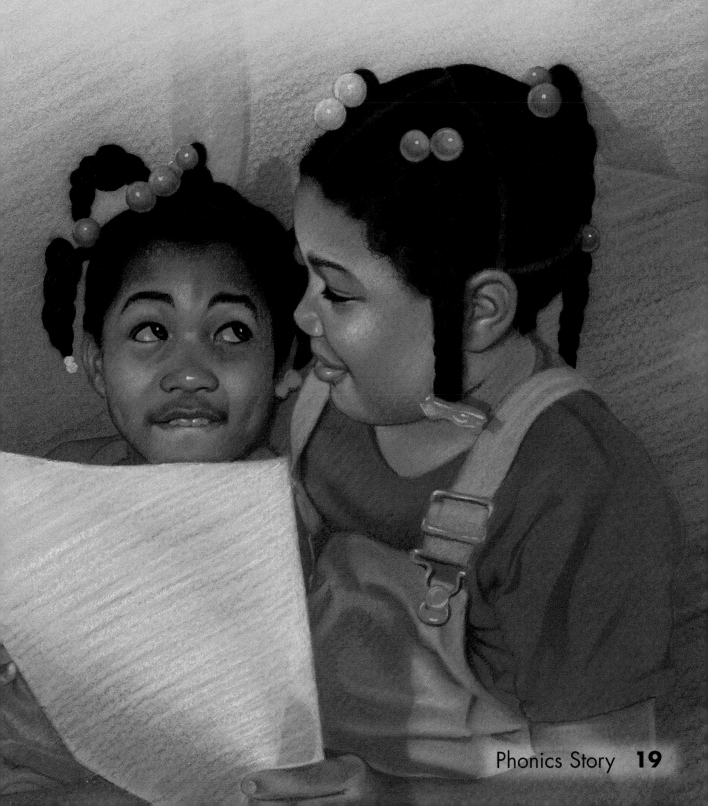

Daddy, Could I Have an Elephant?

by Jake Wolf
illustrated by Marylin Hafner

"Daddy," said Tony. "I need a pet."

"You do?" said his father.

"Yes," said Tony.

"What kind?" said his father.

"Could I have an elephant?" said Tony.

"An elephant?" said his father.
"Where would you keep it?"

"Here in the apartment," said Tony.

"How would you feed it? Where
would it drink?"

"It could drink out of the bathtub,"
said Tony. "We could send out
for Chinese."

"What if it got lonely?" said his father.
"Elephants live in herds."

"We could get another elephant
to keep it company," said Tony.

"How would we move the
elephants up here to the
third floor?" said his father.

"Like pianos," said Tony.
"Pull them on ropes."

"I don't think elephants would fit
through the window," said his father.

"We could try," said Tony.

"What if they got stuck?" said his father.
"People would talk about us."

"What would they say?" said Tony.

"They'd say we're that family with the elephants sticking out the windows."

"Well, how about a python?" said Tony.
"One that's twenty feet long."

"Where would you keep it?"
said his father.

"Some of it on the sofa," said Tony,
"the rest of it on chairs."

"Where would *we* sit?" said his father.

"A flock of woolly sheep would be nice," said Tony. "They could keep us warm at night."

"Sheep go *B-A-A-A* when you're trying to sleep," said his father.

"Not if they're asleep too,"
said Tony. "We could give them
a definite bedtime."

"What if they woke up early?"
said his father.

"I know what," said Tony.

"What?" said his father.

"We could fill the living room with water."

"And then?" said his father.

"We could get a dolphin," said Tony,
"and a baby whale."

"Both?" said his father.

Tony and his father were quiet for a while.

"Maybe we should get something small," said Tony.

"What could that be?" said his father.

"Puppies are small," said Tony.

"Just what I was thinking," said
his father.

About the Author
Jake Wolf

Jake Wolf is the pen name of a famous writer and illustrator of children's books. "Thank you for asking," said Mr. Wolf, "but I don't want anyone to know who I really am."

Mr. Wolf enjoys his privacy. He wants to remain a mystery. What do you think about this?

About the Illustrator
Marylin Hafner

Marylin Hafner has illustrated many books. If you read *Ladybug* magazine, you probably have seen Ms. Hafner's work. She creates stories about a girl named Molly and her cat, Emmett.

Let's Play Together

by Michio Mado

Wouldn't it be nice
If a baby elephant
Came to my house,
Saying, "Let's play together."
Wouldn't it be nice,
Mommy?

Wouldn't it be nice
If a baby bear
Came to my house,
Saying, "Let's play together."
Wouldn't it be nice,
Mommy?

Reader Response

Let's Talk

If you could have any animal from the story as a pet, which one would you choose? Why?

Let's Think

Do the animals really come to Tony's house?

Test Prep
Let's Write

Pretend you are Tony. Write three reasons why you should have a pet.

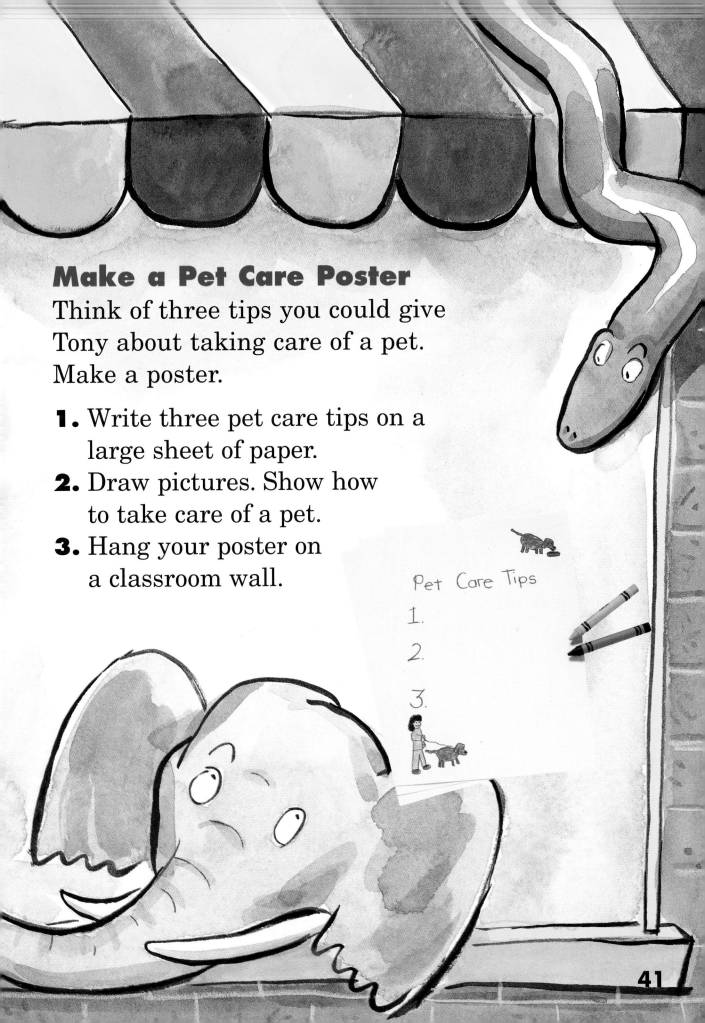

Make a Pet Care Poster

Think of three tips you could give
Tony about taking care of a pet.
Make a poster.

1. Write three pet care tips on a
   large sheet of paper.
2. Draw pictures. Show how
   to take care of a pet.
3. Hang your poster on
   a classroom wall.

Pet Care Tips

1.

2.

3.

Language Arts

Sentences

A **sentence** is a group of words that tells a complete idea. A sentence begins with a capital letter. Many sentences end with a **.**.

The boy plays with the puppy.

This is a sentence. It tells what the boy does.

Talk

Take turns making up sentences about the picture. Tell what each person or animal does.

Write

Match the parts of the sentences. Make sure each sentence makes sense. Write the sentences.

The girl   **swim in the tank.**
The fish   **pays for the puppy.**
Father   **laughs at the puppy.**

Do you own a pet? Have you ever wanted one? Write your own sentences about a pet you would like to own. Use a capital letter at the beginning of each sentence and a **.** at the end. Make sure each sentence tells a complete idea.

The Wobbly People in Ellen's Block House

by David A. Adler

illustrated by Nan Brooks

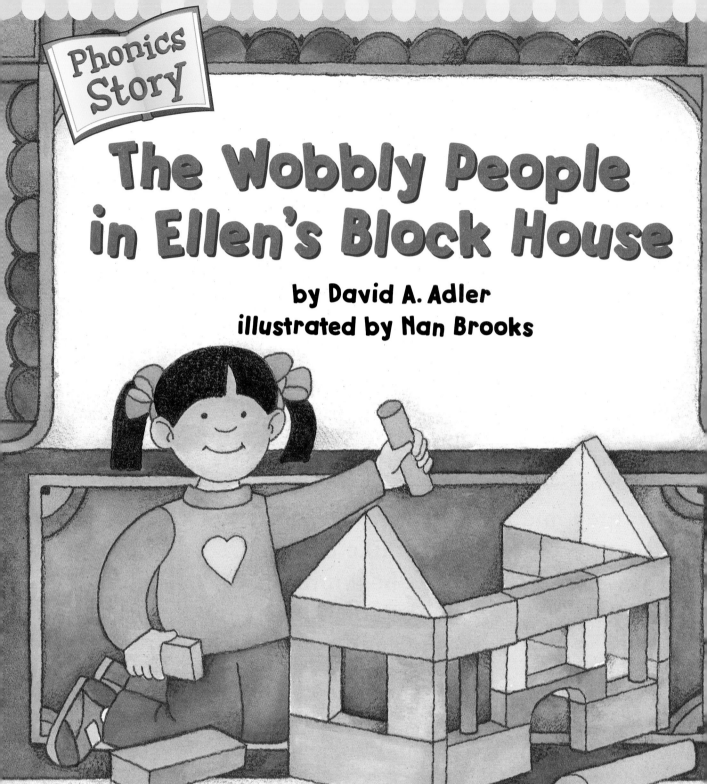

"Look," Ellen told her best friend Peg.

"I made a house of blocks."

"That's great," Peg said.

Peg found some wobbly people. She put
them in the block house. Peg told Ellen,
"These are Don, Bob, Beth, and Jenny.
These are the people who live in your
block house."

Peg played with the wobbly people. She
fed them with a tiny red spoon.

"Here, Don. Taste this. Here, Beth.
Taste this."

Peg made Bob hop and Jenny jog.

Ellen said, "Let me play too."

"No, Peg told her. "They are *my* wobbly people."

"Well," Ellen said. "If I can't play with *your* wobbly people, then *your* wobbly people can't live in *my* block house!"

Peg took Don, Bob, Beth, and Jenny out of Ellen's block house.

Peg looked at her wobbly people. They had nowhere to live.

Ellen looked at the block house she had made. It was empty.

The two best friends looked at each other.

"I'll share my wobbly people with you,"
Peg said.

"And I'll share my block house with you,"
Ellen said.

Later, Peg's mom gave Peg and Ellen pretzels and fresh hot popcorn. "Thank you," Peg and Ellen said. They shared the pretzels and popcorn.

Poppleton and the Grapefruit

by Cynthia Rylant • illustrated by Mark Teague

One day Poppleton was watching TV. The man on TV said grapefruit made people live longer.

Poppleton hated grapefruit. But he wanted to live longer. He wanted to live to be one hundred.

So he went to the store and
brought home some grapefruit.

He cut it up and took a little taste.
Poppleton's lips turned outside-in.

He took another little taste.
Poppleton's eyes made tears.

He took the tiniest taste
he could possibly take.

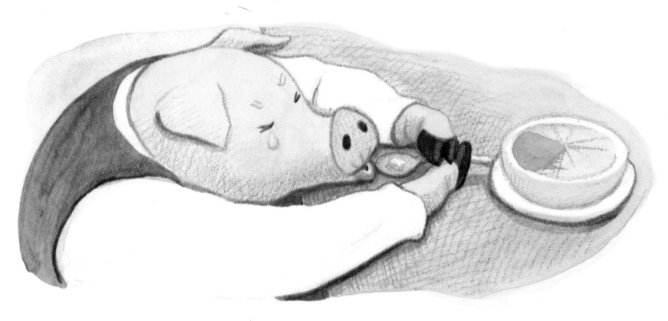

Poppleton's face turned green.

Poppleton's friend Hudson knocked
at the door.

"Poppleton, why are you all green?"
Hudson cried. "And where are
your lips?"

"I am eating grapefruit to live longer,"
said Poppleton. "And it is making
me sick."

"Then don't eat it!" cried Hudson.

"But I want to live to be one hundred,"
said Poppleton.

"With no lips?" asked Hudson.

"What else can I do?" asked Poppleton.

"Wait here," said Hudson.

Soon he was back with a very,
very, very old mouse.

"This is my uncle Bill," said Hudson.
"Uncle Bill, tell Poppleton how you
lived to be one hundred."

Uncle Bill nodded. He leaned
over to Poppleton.

"Friends," he said.

"Friends?" asked Poppleton.

"Friends," said Uncle Bill. "What
did you do with your lips?"

When Uncle Bill and Hudson left,
Poppleton threw all of the
grapefruit away.

And as soon as his lips came back,

he went out to find some friends.

About the Author
Cynthia Rylant

Until she was eight years old, Cynthia Rylant lived in a house with no running water. After college she worked as a waitress. Then she got a job in a library. "And boy, did my life change when I discovered children's books!" she says.

About the Illustrator
Mark Teague

Even as a child, Mark Teague made his own books. When he grew up, he worked in a bookstore. In the store he remembered the fun of making books. He decided to try it again.

"I use a pencil for drawing and a huge eraser for erasing until I get it right," Mr. Teague says.

Reader Response

Let's Think
How could friends help Poppleton live a long life?

Let's Talk
If you could talk to Poppleton, what would you say to him about making new friends?

Test Prep
Let's Write
How can someone make a new friend? Write three ways to meet and keep a new friend.

Make a Collage

Poppleton ate grapefruit because it was good for him. Make a collage about good health.

1. Draw the shape of a person on a large sheet of paper. Cut it out.
2. Find magazines or newspapers. Cut out pictures of healthy foods. Cut out pictures of people doing things that are good for them too.
3. Glue your pictures on the paper.
4. Share your collage with your classmates.

Language Arts

Subjects of Sentences

The **subject** of a sentence tells who or what does something.

Subject
↓

| **The family** | shops for fruit. |
| **The pear** | falls to the ground. |

Talk

Talk about the picture. Name who or what does something. Then use that subject in a complete sentence.

Write

Write the sentences. Underline the subject.

1. The dog wants the pear.
2. The basket holds the fruit.
3. The mother buys grapefruit.

Write your own sentences. Underline the subjects.

The Workers

by B. G. Hennessy
illustrated by
Seymour Chwast

It is time to go to work.
This worker wears
an orange vest and
holds a sign.

This worker keeps many things clean.
He will use a bucket and mop.

This worker wears a white apron. She will use a big spoon and pot.

This worker likes to use a computer.
She talks on the phone.

This worker will make everything ready for the best workers in the world.

Tools

by Ann Morris
photographed by Ken Heyman

A Look at Tools Around the World

Peru

United States

All over the world people use tools.

Tools help us in many ways.

Hong Kong

They help us to cut

and pound

Brazil

Bali

and dig.

Bali

France

We farm with tools.

Peru

We cook with tools.

We even eat with tools!

United States

United States

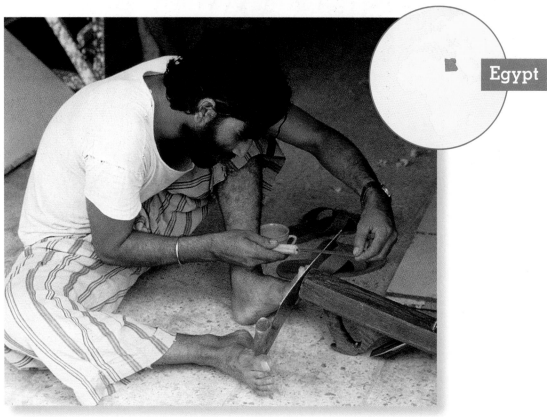

Egypt

People use tools to make things
and to fix things

Portugal

and to clean.

India

Russia

Tools help us to write and count

Salvador

and draw and paint.

Tools help us with our work.

They make our lives easier!

Tools Around the World

Can you find Brazil, Russia, and Egypt?

UNITED STATES

MEXICO

EL SALVADOR

PERU

BRAZIL

N
W · E
S

About the Author and the Photographer

Author

Ann Morris
Ann Morris grew up in New York City. She has always liked learning about people and where they live. She also likes music, cooking, and cats.

Ken Heyman
Ken Heyman grew up in New York City too. He began taking photographs in high school. He still likes to take pictures as he travels.

Photographer

Ann Morris and Ken Heyman have made many books together.

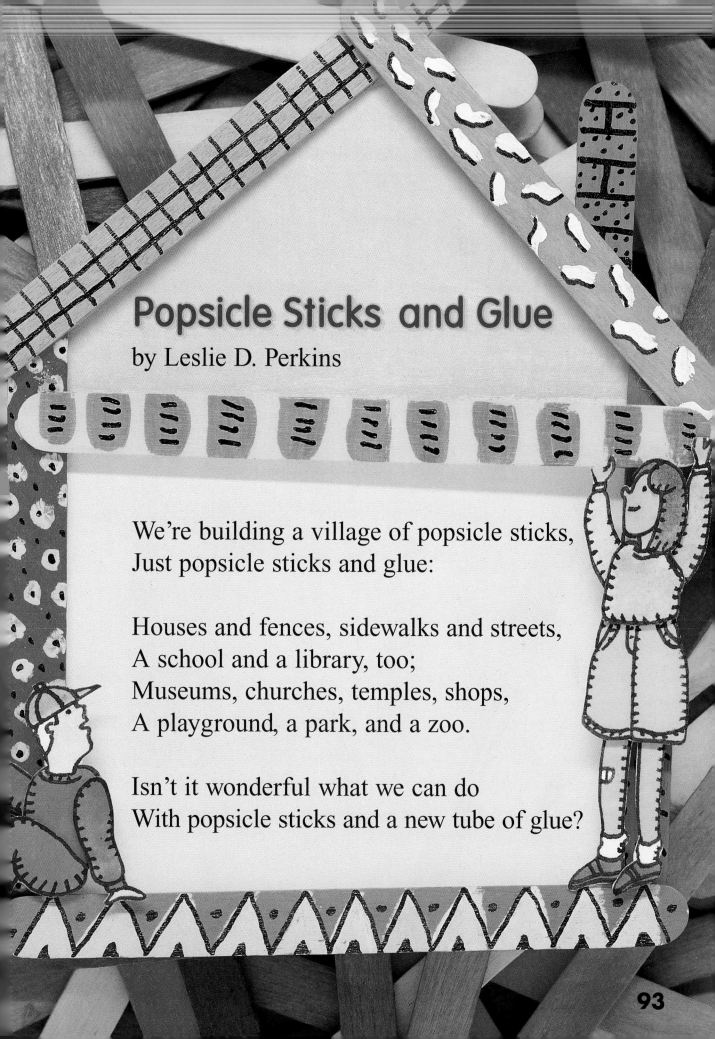

Popsicle Sticks and Glue

by Leslie D. Perkins

We're building a village of popsicle sticks,
Just popsicle sticks and glue:

Houses and fences, sidewalks and streets,
A school and a library, too;
Museums, churches, temples, shops,
A playground, a park, and a zoo.

Isn't it wonderful what we can do
With popsicle sticks and a new tube of glue?

Reader Response

Let's Talk

What tools do you use every day? Why do you need them?

Let's Think

Do people use the same tools everywhere in the world? How do you know?

Test Prep
Let's Write

Think of a tool that you use every day. How do you use it? Write directions for using that tool.

Invent a Tool

Invent a tool that people could use. What would they do with it?

1. Think of a new tool people could use.
2. Draw a picture of it.
3. Find things to make your new tool. You might use:

paper clips	straws
sticks	rubber bands
glue	boxes

4. Try making it and using it.

Predicates of Sentences

A sentence has two parts. The **subject** tells who or what does something. The **predicate** tells what the subject does.

Subject	Predicate
Maria	**measures with her ruler.**
Paul	**colors the box.**

Talk

Tell what the children might do with the tools in the picture. Use sentences. What is the predicate in each sentence?

96

Write

Write the sentences. Underline the predicate.

1. **The children make something.**
2. **The glue dries slowly.**
3. **Maria and Paul will put the straws on top.**

Write your own sentences about making something. Underline the predicates.

The Green Leaf Club
News

by G. Brian Karas

Bike Trip to Green Lake

It is spring and all Green Leaf Club members should get out their bikes! We are planning a trip to Green Lake each week this month. It should be an easy ride.

Meet us at the club each Saturday at 9:00 A.M. Bring a lunch and something to drink. Bring a treat too! The trip should take three hours. See you there!

Our Trip To Eagle Peak

Last year we went to Eagle Peak. It was a very long ride. It was very steep too! We stopped to eat in the shade of some green leaves. Then it started to rain!

We had to rush through our picnic lunch. On the way home, our tires sank deep in the mud. When we got home, we were a very tired bunch!

Bike Safety

It is very busy on the streets this time of year. Have fun on your bikes, but please be careful. Watch out for cars and people. Ride at a safe speed.

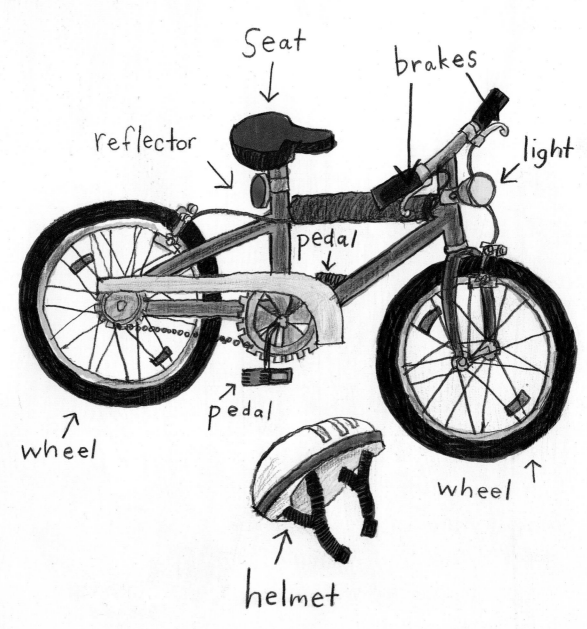

Don't forget these three rules:

1. Always wear a helmet.

2. Test your brakes.

3. Use hand signals to turn, slow down, and stop.

New Bike Trail Opens!

Beaver Creek Trail is opening! A ribbon will be cut to open it. We will thank the people for their hard work. After that, we will leave for a trail ride.

The new trail is three miles long. It goes through hills and by a creek. We should see lots of beavers along the way. Would you like to join us?

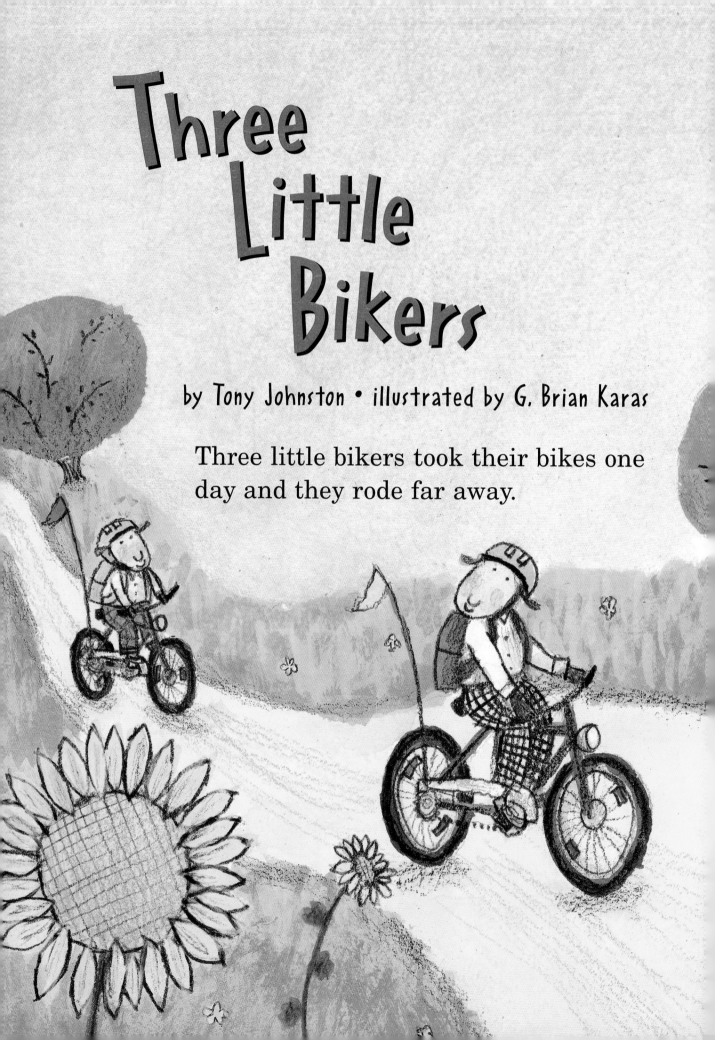

Three Little Bikers

by Tony Johnston • illustrated by G. Brian Karas

Three little bikers took their bikes one day and they rode far away.

The grass was green. The trees were too.
And the sky was blue
as they rode
with their packs on their backs
and three little flags that went
flap, flap, flap
in the wind.

Wind blew in their hair.
It blew everywhere
and puffed their shirts
like little white sails.
And it tickled,
so they giggled
as they rode
with their packs on their backs
and three little flags that went
flap, flap, flap
in the wind.

They rode through gravel
ping, ping, ping.
They rode through dust.
Whisssssh!
They rode through grass
and left their tracks
like three quick little snakes.

They came to a gully,
steep and deep.
Should they? Could they?
Would they cross?
Yes! Yes! Yes!

Watch for Hill

They raced down the gully
and up again
with their packs on their backs
and three little flags that went
flap, flap, flap
in the wind.

They came to a puddle,
fat with rain.
Should they? Could they?
Would they cross?
Yes! Yes! Yes!

Whooosh!
They splashed
a shiny silver spray.
Then they raced away.

They came to a hill,
green and high.
Should they? Would they?
Could they climb?
Yes! Yes! Yes!

They crept up the hill
with their packs on their backs
and three little flags that went
flop, flop, flop.
Like three little turtles
hurrying up.

Picnic Area
Ahead

At the very top
they shouted, "Here we are!"
And a voice just like
a voice in a jar
shouted "Are! Are! Are!"

"Are"

"Are"

Here We Are

"Are"

Picnic
Area

A bird flew up.
So they flew too
and soared like birds
all over the hill
with their arms like wings that went
flap, flap, flap
in the wind.

They rolled all over
like rolling stones.
Grass stuck in their hair.
It stuck everywhere.
And it tickled,
so they giggled
as they rolled.

Then they flopped in the grass
and ate—*chomp, chomp, chomp*—
like three hungry little ants,
till their lunch was gone.
They blew into their bags
and popped them—
Bang! Bang! Bang!

And they sang a loud song
like popping bags,
and they sang a soft song
like birds

till the day got old
and the sky got red
and they knew
it was time to leave.

They looked over the hill,
far, FAR, FAR.
Should they? Could they?
Would they go?
Yes! Yes! Yes!

So—
three little bikers raced down again
with their packs on their backs
and three little flags that went
flap, flap, flap
in the wind.

Gully

Puddle

Hill

As they rode
they sang a song.
And as night came on
their headlights glowed
like three little fireflies
all the way home.

Home

About the Author

Tony Johnston

Tony Johnston was a teacher. She wrote stories for the children in her class. Then she decided to write books for all children to read. Ms. Johnston likes to write in her family room with her dog, Suzi, on her feet!

About the Illustrator

G. Brian Karas

An art teacher helped G. Brian Karas realize that he could be an artist. Since then, he has illustrated over fifty books for children. He believes that creating books "is the most worthwhile thing I can do."

Mr. Karas once was an artist for a large greeting card company.

I Like to Ride My Bike

by Lori Marie Carlson

I'm ready
for a bike ride. I wear
long blue shorts, my red helmet and
a white T-shirt hanging to my knees.
One pedal
spins
and then, I'm off!

Leaves blur into green air
people shout hello, be careful
stay on the sidewalk.

The wind cools my arms
and legs.
I feel free.

Reader Response

Let's Talk
What part of the three little bikers' trip looks the most fun? Why?

Let's Think
The three little bikers ride up and down hills. How would the story change if they rode where you live?

Test Prep
Let's Write
Write about something special you have done with friends. Tell what you did first, next, and last.

Make a Map

Look back at the story. Find all the places the bikers went. Make a map to show the bikers' trip.

1. Make a list of all the places you want to show on your map.
2. Draw a bike trail on a large sheet of paper.
3. Add pictures of the places.
4. Draw arrows to show which way the bikers traveled.
5. Color your map.

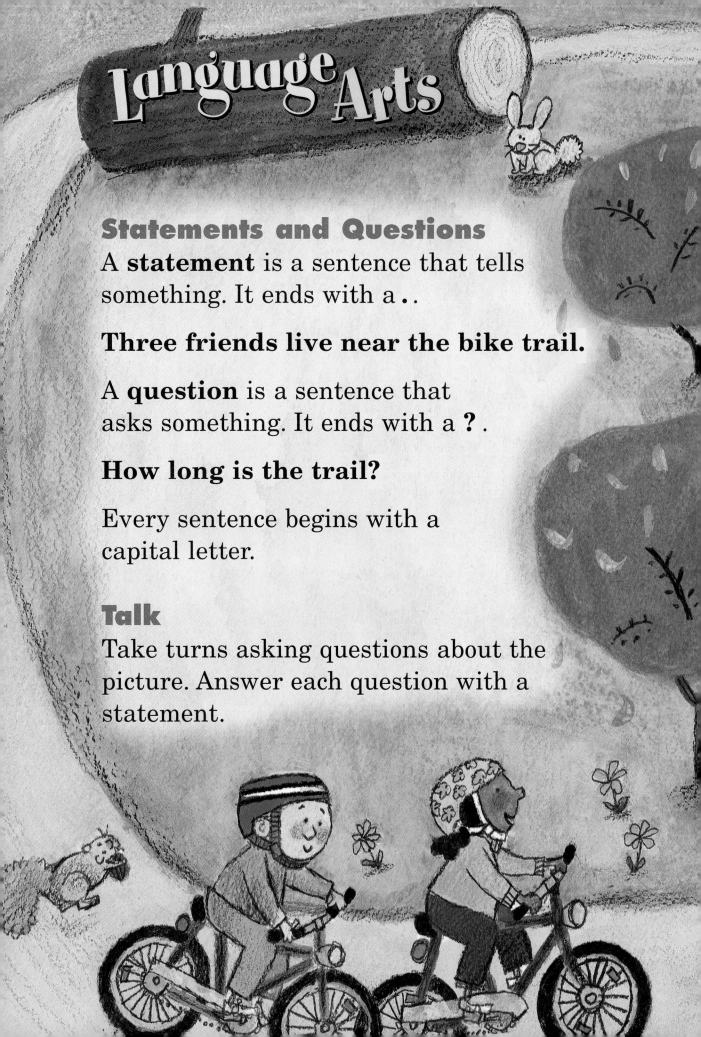

Language Arts

Statements and Questions

A **statement** is a sentence that tells something. It ends with a **.**.

Three friends live near the bike trail.

A **question** is a sentence that asks something. It ends with a **?**.

How long is the trail?

Every sentence begins with a capital letter.

Talk

Take turns asking questions about the picture. Answer each question with a statement.

Write

Write the sentences. Use a **.** or a **?** at the end of each sentence.

1. **Where are the apples___**
2. **The boy has a red bike___**
3. **Who will carry the apples___**
4. **The leaves are falling___**

Draw a picture of your favorite outdoor place. Read each question below and answer with a statement.

• Where is your favorite place?
• What do you see at this place?
• What do you like to do there?

131

House Repair

by Joanne Ryder
illustrated by Carla Siboldi

Lena and Cory were busy. They were completing their birdhouses for art class.

"These will be great!" said Lena.

Lena was in a big hurry. She wanted to show off her birdhouse. Lena did not see the backpacks on the ground.

Lena walked right into a backpack
and fell.

"Are you okay?" Cory asked.

"I am okay," said Lena, "but my
house is not."

Cory said, "Give it to me." She took
the house and put it on her lap.

Cory and Lena went to art class.
"I will never be able to repair my house," said Lena.
"Do not worry," said Cory. "We will fix your house."

Cory took off the crushed parts. Then she got busy. She cut and painted and fixed.

"Is this okay?" Cory asked.

"It is more than okay," said Lena.

"These are all really great," said
their teacher.

"Yes, they are," Lena whispered to
Cory. "And so are you!"

The Surprise

by Arnold Lobel

It was October.

The leaves had fallen off

the trees.

They were lying on the ground.

"I will go to Toad's house,"

said Frog.

"I will rake all of the leaves

that have fallen on his lawn.

Toad will be surprised."

Frog took a rake
out of the garden shed.
Toad looked out of his window.
"These messy leaves
have covered everything," said Toad.
He took a rake out of the closet.
"I will run over to Frog's house.
I will rake all of his leaves.
Frog will be very pleased."

Frog ran through the woods
so that Toad would not see him.

Toad ran through the high grass
so that Frog would not see him.

Frog came to Toad's house.

He looked in the window.

"Good," said Frog.

"Toad is out.

He will never know

who raked his leaves."

Toad got to Frog's house.

He looked in the window.

"Good," said Toad.

"Frog is not home.

He will never guess

who raked his leaves."

Frog worked hard.

He raked the leaves into a pile.

Soon Toad's lawn was clean.

Frog picked up his rake

and started home.

Toad pushed and pulled on the rake.

He raked the leaves into a pile.

Soon there was not a single leaf

in Frog's front yard.

Toad took his rake

and started home.

A wind came.

It blew across the land.

The pile of leaves

that Frog had raked for Toad

blew everywhere.

The pile of leaves

that Toad had raked for Frog

blew everywhere.

When Frog got home,
he said, "Tomorrow I will
clean up the leaves
that are all over my own lawn.
How surprised Toad must be!"

When Toad got home,
he said, "Tomorrow I will
get to work and rake
all of my own leaves.
How surprised Frog must be!"

That night
Frog and Toad
were both happy
when they each
turned out the light
and went to bed.

About the Author
Arnold Lobel

Arnold Lobel wrote and illustrated almost one hundred books. "One of the secrets of writing good books for children is that you must write books for yourself," he once said.

Watching his children catch frogs and toads one summer gave Mr. Lobel the idea for the characters Frog and Toad. Mr. Lobel said, "I loved those little creatures."

Reader Response

Let's Talk
Was the ending a surprise? Why or why not?

Let's Think
Why are Frog and Toad happy at the end of the story?

Test Prep
Let's Write
Think of something nice that someone has done for you. Write a thank-you note to that person.

Act it Out

Act out a new ending for the story. Work with a friend.

1. Pretend that the wind had not blown Frog and Toad's leaves around. Talk about how the story might have ended.
2. Practice acting out your new ending.
3. Make Frog and Toad masks.
4. Act out your new ending for classmates. Wear your masks.

Language Arts

Commands and Exclamations

A **command** is a sentence that tells you to do something. It ends with a **.** .

Rake the leaves.

In every command the subject is *you*, but *you* is not usually shown.

An **exclamation** is a sentence that shows surprise or strong feelings. It ends with an **!** .

I love to jump in the leaves!

Every sentence begins with a capital letter.

Talk

Look at the picture. Tell what each person is saying to the other. Use commands and exclamations.

Write

Write the sentences. Use a **.**
or an **!** at the end of each sentence.

1. Make a neat pile of leaves___
2. We can't wait to play in
   the leaves___
3. It is a great big mess____

Write sentences about things you
do at school. Use commands and
exclamations.

153

Franny and Ginny

Daddy, Could I Have an Elephant?

apartment

could

elephant

have

need

pianos

quiet

then

The Wobbly People in Ellen's Block House

Poppleton and the Grapefruit

hundred

knocked

outside

sick

taste

tears

The Green Leaf Club News

The Workers

Tools

clean

easier

farm

fix

tools

use

world

write

Three Little Bikers

climb

everywhere

giggled

should

spray

through

House Repair

The Surprise

guess

house

never

pile

pleased

surprised

tomorrow

Test Talk

Understand the Question

You must understand a test question before you can answer it. Think about what the question is asking. What do you need to find out?

A test about "Poppleton and the Grapefruit" may have this question.

1. What happened to Poppleton's lips after he ate the grapefruit?

Ⓐ They turned green.

Ⓑ They turned outside-in.

Ⓒ They became swollen.

Read the question. What is the question asking? What do you need to find out?

Here is how one boy chose his answer.

I need to find out what happened to Poppleton's lips after he ate the grapefruit. I remember that his lips didn't turn green or swollen. The answer is B.

Try it!

What do you need to find out to answer this question about "Poppleton and the Grapefruit."

2. Who tells Poppleton that friends will help him live longer?

(A) **Uncle Bill**

(B) **the TV**

(C) **Hudson**

Zoom In!

What can we learn from looking at the world around us?

The Ugly Duckling

by Hans Christian Andersen • retold by Sharon Fear
illustrated by Cheryl Kirk Noll

Mother Duck watches. Her five eggs
are hatching. Four new little
ducklings hatch first. Then one big
duckling hatches.

"Four are quite pretty," said Mother Duck. "But this big one looks very plain."

"He is an ugly color," said Hen.

"He has ugly feet," added Goose.

"He is ugly all over," said Dog.

"I must be very ugly," said the duckling. "I will not be able to stay. I will go and live by myself."

So the ugly duckling ran away.

His days were sad. He had no one

to play with. His nights were cold.

He had no one to keep him warm.

But time passes.

One day he saw three pretty birds.

They were floating his way.

"Look!" said Hen. "Swans!"

"Beautiful swans!" said Goose.

"Four beautiful swans!" said Dog.

The ugly duckling looks in the water.

He sees . . . four beautiful swans!

And he is one of them!

DUCK

by Angela Royston
photographed by Barrie Watts

In the nest

My mother has laid her eggs
in this nest. She sits on
them to keep them warm.

Inside each egg a new duckling
is growing. This one is me. I am
just beginning to hatch.

Just hatched

I have chipped away my shell,
and now I am pushing myself out.

At last I am out of my shell.

I can see, hear, stand, and walk.
I can cheep too. Where
is my mother?

First swim

I am two days old now. I am going to the pond for my first swim.

As soon as I am in the water, I start to swim.

I use my webbed feet to paddle through the water.

Feeding

I am one week old and
getting bigger. I like to
explore everything.

This bowl has wet mud in it.
I search the mud with my
beak for things to eat.

Look! I've jumped right
into the bowl.

In the water

I am two weeks old,
and I love to swim
in the water.
I look for things to
eat on the surface.

I shake the water off my body.

New feathers

I am three weeks old.
My yellow down is
falling out, and new
white feathers are
beginning to grow.

I stay close to the other
ducklings.
Our mother watches
out for danger.

Sometimes we huddle together. Our feathers help to keep us warm.

Nearly grown up

I am six weeks old and
nearly grown up.

All my feathers are white,
and my wings are big
and strong.

See how much I have
grown. This bowl is small,
but it seemed big when
I first jumped into it.

See how I grew

The egg

One hour old

Two days old

Seven days old

Two weeks old

Three weeks old   Six weeks old

About the Author
Angela Royston

Angela Royston has written many animal stories. She often writes about farm animals. Ms. Royston learns a lot when she writes. "I always become interested in the subjects of the books I work on," she says.

About the Photographer
Barrie Watts

Barrie Watts spends time in Great Britain. The pictures Watts takes are often of animals and plants. They appear in many books and magazines. The subjects of books by Barrie Watts can be as tiny as a fly or a honeybee or as large as a redwood tree.

Baby Chick

by Aileen Fisher

Peck
    peck
        peck

on the warm brown egg.
OUT comes a neck.
OUT comes a leg.

How
does
a chick,
who's not been about,
discover the trick
of how to get out?

Reader Response

Let's Talk

Which week in the duck's life was the most interesting? Why?

Let's Think

Compare the duck at two weeks old and at six weeks old. What has changed?

Test Prep
Let's Write

Duck tells his story about growing up. Tell your own story. Write sentences about what you were like growing up.

Make a Chart

How can you tell a duck's age? Make a chart that shows three stages in a duck's life.

1. Divide a large sheet of paper into three parts.
2. Choose three stages in a duck's life to write about.
3. Write sentences about each stage on each part of the paper.
4. Draw pictures that go with what you wrote.

1. The baby duck is about to hatch. The egg is cracked.

2. The duck is one week old and can fit in a bowl.

3. The duck is six weeks old and is white. The duck cannot fit in a bowl anymore.

185

Nouns

A **noun** is a word that names a person, place, animal, or thing.

The **eggs** hatch by the **pond.**

The **boy** watches the **duck.**

What does each noun name?

person	place	animal	thing
boy	pond	duck	eggs

Talk

Talk about the picture. What words are nouns? Where will each noun go on the chart?

Write

Write the sentences. Find the nouns. Above each noun, draw a picture of the word.

1. The girl feeds the ducks.
2. The egg cracks open.
3. The ducks swim in the pond.

Write your own sentences. Use nouns. Draw a picture of each noun.

Eye Spy

by Pat Cummings
illustrated by Chris Powers

Mrs. Bright waited for the whole class to quiet down. "Thank you, Dwight," she said. "My, your frog farm was very nice. Now, I have an idea. Why don't you carry your frog farm outside? The frogs might like it there."

"OK," said Dwight. "I might find them some bugs first. My frogs *love* to eat bugs."

Mrs. Bright smiled. Then she said, "All right. Who is next? Ida?"

Ida had to carry her things slowly because she wanted to keep some of them hidden. She knew everyone would try to peek. Ida put three pictures up against the board. She put a bag on the floor nearby.

"Try to guess what each picture is,"
Ida said to the whole class. "I don't think
you will get them right," she giggled.

"Number one is really easy," Myra said. "It is just dry dirt."

"Number two is simple," said Simon. "Those are little glass blocks."

Dwight got up because he wanted a closer look. "Why, number three is a fuzzy cotton ball!" he said.

Ida picked up the bag. She pulled out a hand lens and a telescope.

Ida held the hand lens over her arm.
"This goes with number one."

"My, oh my!" said Michael. "This is
not dirt. This is skin really close up!"

Next Ida took out a packet of sugar.
She put some under the class microscope.

"Hey!" laughed Simon. "The glass
blocks are really bits of sugar!"

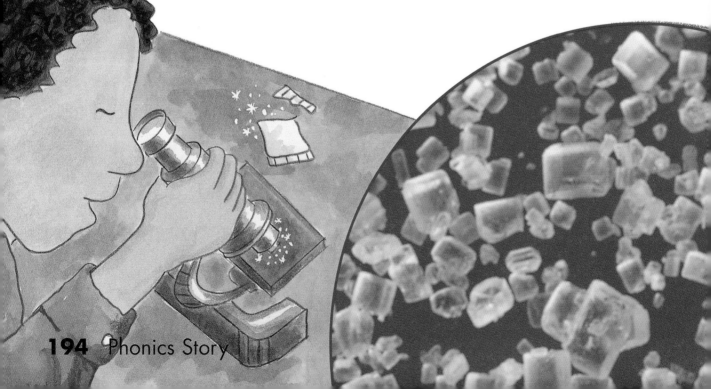

"Now, this goes with number three," said Ida. She pointed the telescope out the window. "Tell me what you see, Dwight."

"Yikes!" yelled Dwight. "I see my whole frog farm about to run across the playground!"

Seeing

by Joanna Cole
illustrated by Neesa Becker

Is your eyeball really a ball? Yes! Most of your eye is hidden inside your skull.

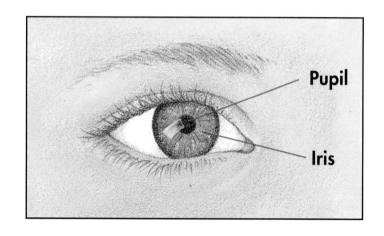

Here is what your whole eye looks like. Each of your eyes has an opening to let in light. That opening is called the pupil.

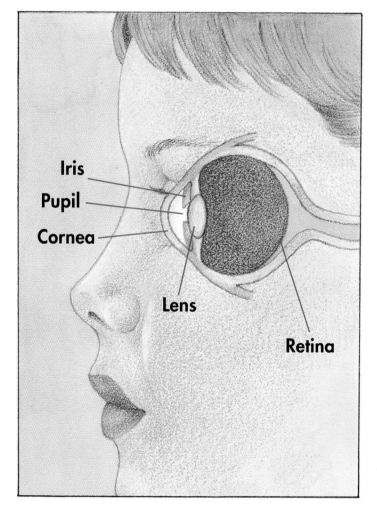

Try This

Dim the lights.

Look at your eyes in a mirror.

Are your pupils big?

Now turn on a bright light.

Did you see your pupils get smaller?

Your pupils get bigger and smaller to let in just the right amount of light.

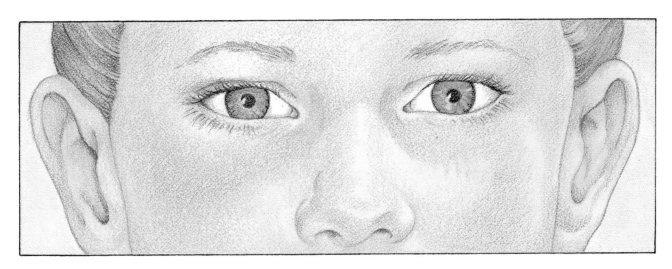

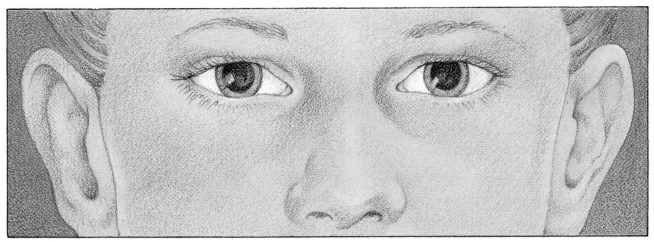

Your eyes are made to see.

How do they work?

Look at a hat.

Light bounces off the hat and goes into your eye.

The light hits the back of your eyeball.

A picture of the hat is made there.

Nerves—like wires—carry
messages about the picture
from the back of your eye
to special places in your brain.
You need your brain *and* your
eyes to see.

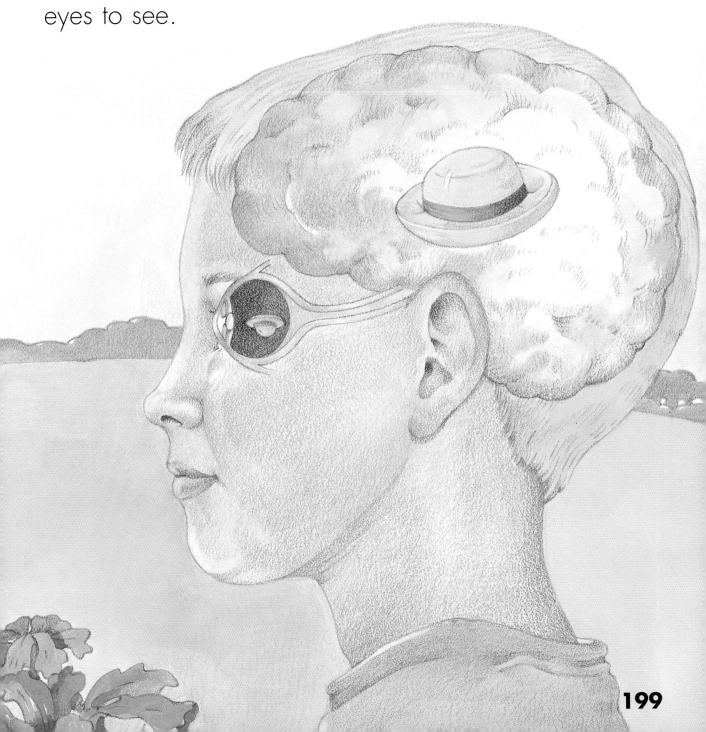

Sometimes your eyes see things
that don't make sense.
Then your brain tries
to make sense of them.

Try This

You see a friend coming down the street.
While he is still far away, hold up your
thumb. Your eyes say that he looks
smaller than your thumb! But your brain
is not fooled. Your friend only looks small
because he is far away. You know that
he is still big.

Sometimes you *can* fool your brain.

Try This

Look at the picture. Which tree is bigger?
Did you say the one on the right?
No! Both are the same size.
Measure them and see.
Why does one tree seem bigger?
Because the artist drew the picture with lines that
make the tree on the right seem farther away.
Your brain acts the way it did when you saw
your friend down the street. It tells you the tree
on the right is bigger than it really is.

Sometimes you can see two pictures in one.

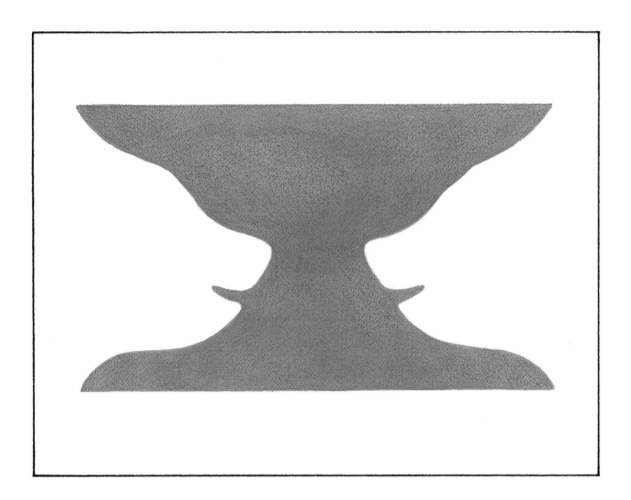

In this picture, do you see a green vase? Or do you see two white dogs looking at each other? You may see one picture, and then the other. But your brain cannot see both pictures at once.

About the Author
Joanna Cole

Joanna Cole began writing stories when she was a child. She also enjoyed drawing pictures to go with her stories.

Ms. Cole always loved writing about science more than anything else. Today, she is well known for her science books. In fact, she is the author of the Magic School Bus books.

Reader Response

Let's Talk
Have your eyes
ever fooled you?
Tell about it.

Let's Think
What would happen
if your pupils did not
get bigger or smaller?

Test Prep
Let's Write
Pretend that you are a teacher. You
are teaching your class something
about eyes. Write what you will
say first, next, and last.

Look Closely

Look around you! What do you see?
Look at things close up.

1. Use a hand lens if you have one.
2. Walk around your classroom, outdoors,
   or at home. Look through the lens.
3. Draw a picture of something you see.
   On the back of the picture, write what
   you are looking at.
4. Show the picture to classmates.
   Ask them to guess what you were
   looking at.

Proper Nouns

Special names for people, places, and animals are called **proper nouns.** Proper nouns begin with capital letters.

The girl lost her ball in **Central Park.**

The boy helped **Oscar** and **Liz** find it.

What are the proper nouns in each sentence?

Talk

Look at the picture. What proper nouns might you find? Use each one in a sentence.

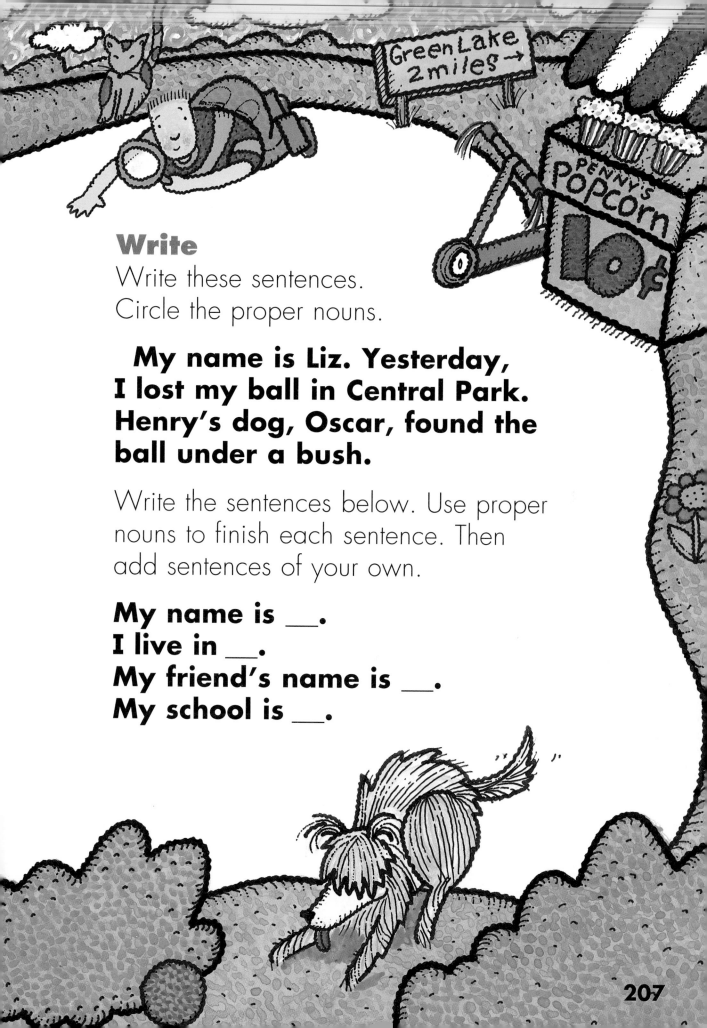

Write

Write these sentences.
Circle the proper nouns.

My name is Liz. Yesterday, I lost my ball in Central Park. Henry's dog, Oscar, found the ball under a bush.

Write the sentences below. Use proper nouns to finish each sentence. Then add sentences of your own.

My name is __.
I live in __.
My friend's name is __.
My school is __.

Furry Mouse

by Kana Riley
photographed by John Moore

At first, it is dark inside the box.
Furry Mouse looks around. All she
can see is a little light that shines
through holes in the lid.

Then the lid opens. Light comes in. Furry Mouse opens her eyes wide and turns.

Furry Mouse wiggles her nose.

She smells food—seeds, carrots,

and one other thing. She wiggles

her nose again. Strawberries! Yum!

Furry Mouse loves strawberries.

Something stirs. Furry Mouse perks up her ears. What does she hear?

Furry Mouse looks one way, then another. She creeps ahead until she is almost out of the box.

Wood chips brush over her fur.

They feel good under her paws.

She looks around her new home.

Look! It has a water bottle and a dish for food. This is perfect.

Furry Mouse is thirsty. But first she must look around some more.

Something stirs again! Furry Mouse turns to look. A ball of fur races up the ladder. It is another mouse! He jumps down and almost lands on Furry Mouse.

He scurries around and under the wood chips.

Then he hops up on the wheel.

He moves around and around.

Furry Mouse watches. It looks like

fun! She waits for her turn.

Yes, this is a good home.

TWO MICE

by Lynn Reiser

Once there were two mice
who lived beside a window.

One lived
inside the window,
in a cage on top of a
bookshelf.
One lived outside
the window,
in a mouse hole
under a rosebush.

The inside mouse
ate mouse food from a bowl,
drank water from a bottle,
and ran around a wheel.

The outside mouse
ate strawberries
and acorns,
drank raindrops
from rose leaves,
and ran
in and out
the mouse hole
and up and down
and around
the rosebush.

One night
the window was open.
The outside mouse ran in.

The two mice
ate mouse food from the bowl,
drank water from the bottle,
and ran around the wheel.

One mouse
was content.
One mouse was
ready for more.

The outside mouse ran out.
The inside mouse followed.

The two mice ate a strawberry—
and a snake almost ate them.

They nibbled an acorn—and a raccoon
almost nibbled them.

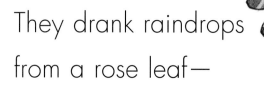
They drank raindrops
from a rose leaf—

and an owl almost
carried them off to her nest.

One mouse
was ready for more.
One mouse
was ready for a nap.

The window was open.
The inside mouse ran in.

The outside mouse
did not follow.
The outside mouse ran
in and out
and up and down
and around,
playing
"catch me if you can"
with the snake
and the raccoon
and the owl.

The inside mouse
took a nap.

MORAL

What thrills one
tires another.

Lynn Reiser

Lynn Reiser likes animals. She likes to write about animals too. In fact, she has written many animal stories. You may enjoy reading her other books about cats and dogs. Ms. Reiser also likes to paint. She painted the pictures for the story *Two Mice*.

Mice

by Rose Fyleman

I think mice
Are rather nice.
    Their tails are long,
    Their faces small,
    They haven't any
    Chins at all.
    Their ears are pink,
    Their teeth are white,
    They run about
    The house at night.
    They nibble things
    They shouldn't touch
    And no one seems
    To like them much.
But I think mice
Are nice.

Reader Response

Let's Talk
Would you rather be the outside mouse or the inside mouse? Why?

Let's Think
What might happen if the inside mouse had to stay outside and the outside mouse had to stay inside?

Test Prep
Let's Write
The outside mouse and the inside mouse each like their own homes best. Write sentences that describe your own special place.

Make a Diorama

Make a home for a mouse. Make it look like an inside home or an outside home.

1. Find a small box.
2. Choose a mouse.
3. Color the inside of the box.
4. Find things to put in the box.
5. Show your mouse's home to others. Can they guess which mouse would live there?

Language Arts

Singular and Plural Nouns

A **singular noun** names one person, place, animal, or thing.

One **lion** sleeps.

Some nouns name more than one. A noun that names more than one is called a **plural noun**. Add **–s** to most nouns to name more than one.

Two **lions** sit in the sun.

Add **–es** to a noun that ends in **s, ch, sh,** or **x** to name more than one.

The **benches** at the beach are hot.

Talk

Find singular and plural nouns in the pictures. Make a list.

Write

Write the sentences. Make the noun plural. Then use it in the sentence. Watch for the **–s** or **–es** ending.

1. The ___ are big. (glass)
2. The lions drink from ___. (cup)

Write sentences about where you live and what you like to do. Use singular and plural nouns from the box.

Nouns

lunches

street

neighbors

friends

bushes

home

bed

buses

boxes

229

The Old Gollywampus

by Toby Speed
illustrated by Mary Grand Pré

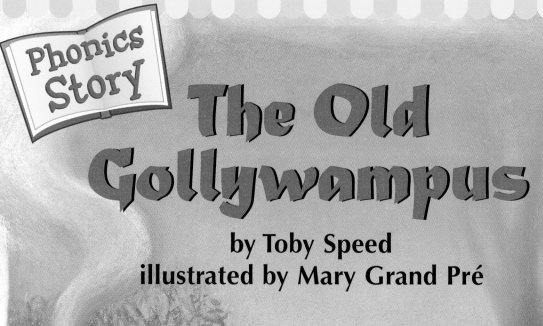

Snake hid low in the woodpile, between rows of oak trees. She was curled in an O. Snake smelled something new. It was not a mouse. It was not a toad.

This smell was cold and crisp.

"It must be the Old Gollywampus!" thought Snake.

She shook all over. All the animals knew about the Old Gollywampus.

The Old Gollywampus was fat and white and as old as the dinosaurs. It came when snakes were sleeping. Only a few animals had seen it—and that was so many years ago.

"I will know it when I see it," Snake told herself.

Slowly, she slid out of the woodpile. The backyard was so cold. She knew that the beast was nearby!

Snake looked up. Snow was blowing everywhere. Was that the Old Gollywampus floating in the wind?

Why was her tail so cold? Snake looked behind her. Sitting on her tail was the Old Gollywampus!

Before it could swallow her, Snake hid.

Snake felt so tired. She curled in an O below the woodpile. The wind was blowing. Snowflakes were floating between the oak trees. Snake slept.

Snakes

by Patricia Demuth
illustrated by Judith Moffatt

Long, long ago, before people knew how to write, they drew pictures on cave walls—pictures of animals.

About a million different animals lived on Earth then. But cave people drew only a few of them.

The snake was one.

People have always found snakes
interesting. Why? Maybe it is their shape.
Snakes have no arms or legs.

Or maybe it is how they move. Snakes
slither and slide on their bellies.

Or maybe it is their skin. Snake skin is
made up of lots of little scales. Most
snake skin looks slimy, but it isn't. It is
very dry.

There are over 2,400 kinds of snakes in the world. They come in many sizes.

The smallest is the thread snake—no bigger than a worm. The giant of all snakes is the anaconda. (You say it like this: an/ə kon/də.) It can be as long as a school bus and weigh as much as two grown men.

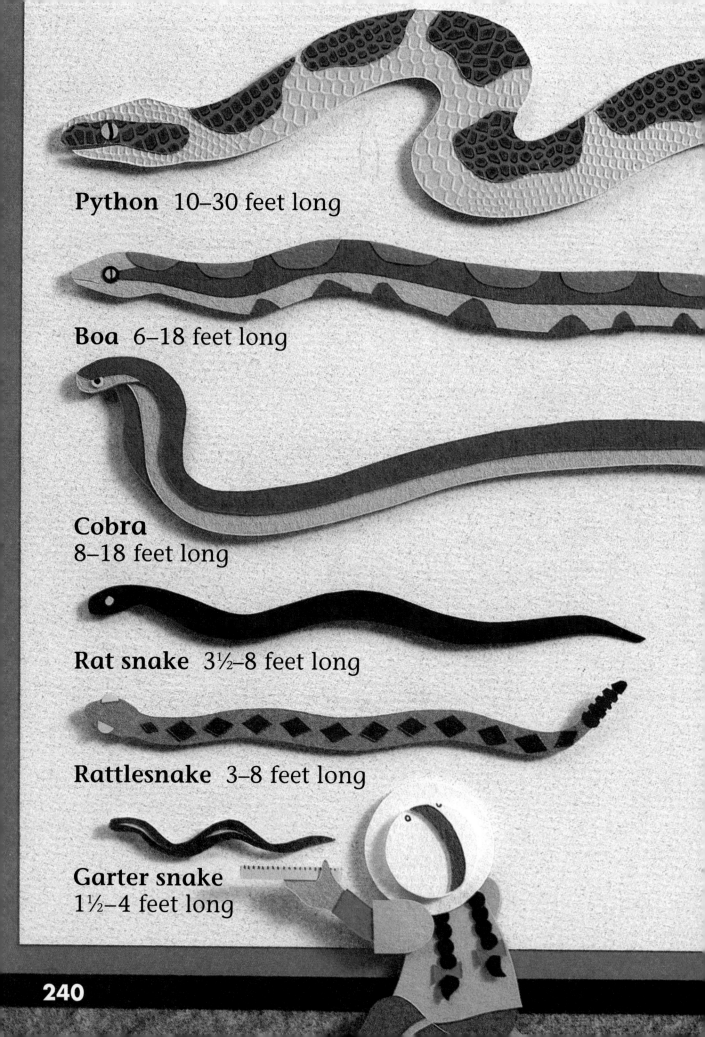

Python 10–30 feet long

Boa 6–18 feet long

Cobra
8–18 feet long

Rat snake 3½–8 feet long

Rattlesnake 3–8 feet long

Garter snake
1½–4 feet long

Other snakes are somewhere in between.

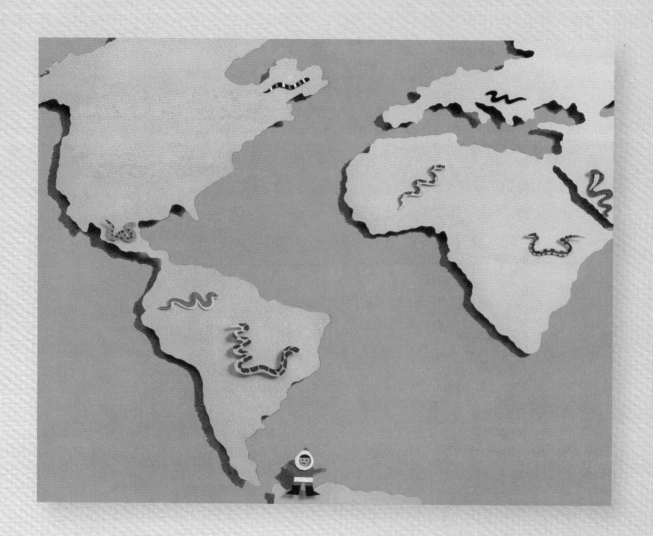

Snakes live almost everywhere: On land, in trees, and underground. In the oceans and lakes.

But snakes don't live near the North Pole or the South Pole. A snake's body can't make its own heat like yours can. So, cold air, cold snake.

But if the air is nice and warm, then the snake is nice and warm too.

Many kinds of snakes can live through cold winters.

How? They find a warm place to hide—in a deep hole, in a cave, or under rocks. Then they go into a deep winter sleep. Here they stay until warm weather returns.

Even when snakes sleep, their eyes are always open. That's because they have no eyelids. A clear cap covers each eye.

Most snakes don't see very well. They can tell if something moves. But this garter snake can barely see the frog that is sitting so quiet and still.

Ribbit, ribbit.
The frog croaks. The garter snake cannot hear the frog. Snakes have no outer ears.

The garter snake flicks its tongue in and out. Suddenly it can smell the frog!

Snakes pick up smells from the air with their tongues. A snake flicking its tongue is like you sniffing with your nose!

That frog must get away fast!

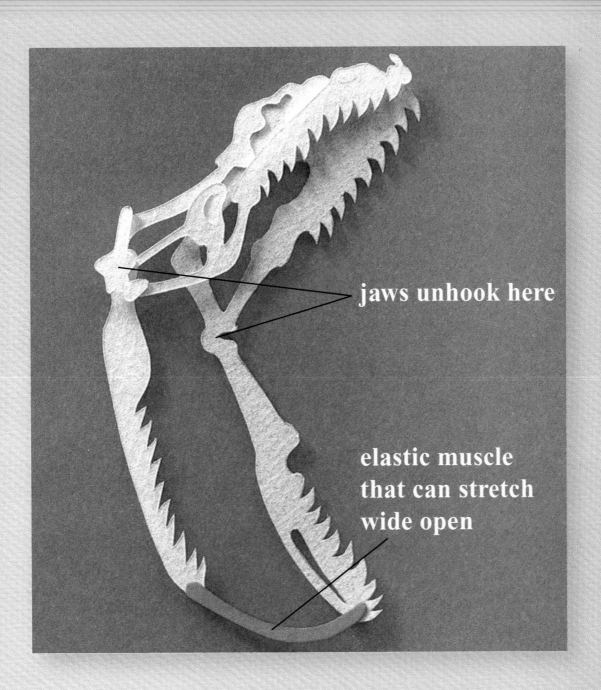

jaws unhook here

elastic muscle
that can stretch
wide open

Snakes do not chew their food. They
swallow it whole by "unhooking"
their jaws.

A python can swallow a whole pig in
one bite.

The coral snake rubs its head on a rock.
Rubbing breaks open the old skin.

Slowly, slowly, the snake crawls out.
Snakes shed their skins two or three times
each year.

A new skin is all grown underneath.
The old skin is worn out. The old skin
peels off. It comes off inside out, like
a T-shirt pulled over your head.

Snakes protect themselves in many ways.
A rattlesnake rattles its tail to make a
loud warning: *Ch-ch-ch-ch-ch!*

The boa curls up into a ball. An enemy can bite its tail. But the boa's head is still safe.

A cottonmouth opens its mouth very, very wide. Enemies flee from the scary sight.

An angry cobra scares away enemies too. It rears up high. It makes its neck big and flat. It jabs forward and gives a loud, sharp *hiss!*

People are often scared of snakes. And yet snakes help people. They kill rats and mice that eat crops.

And snake poison is used for medicine. Experts "milk" the fangs to get out the drops.

People may fear snakes—or they may like them.

But one thing is certain. Snakes have been around for millions and millions and millions of years.

Way before people, there were snakes. Even back in the time of dinosaurs there were snakes.

Snakes are here to stay!

About the Author

Patricia Demuth

Patricia Demuth loved being outdoors when she was a child. She remembers having "time to explore" with her eight brothers and sisters. She still has "great fun" exploring nature and writing about what she finds.

Reader Response

Let's Talk

What are three surprising things you learned about snakes?

Let's Think

How do snakes protect themselves?

Test Prep
Let's Write

Think about what you learned about snakes. Write a poem about a snake. Tell it to a friend.

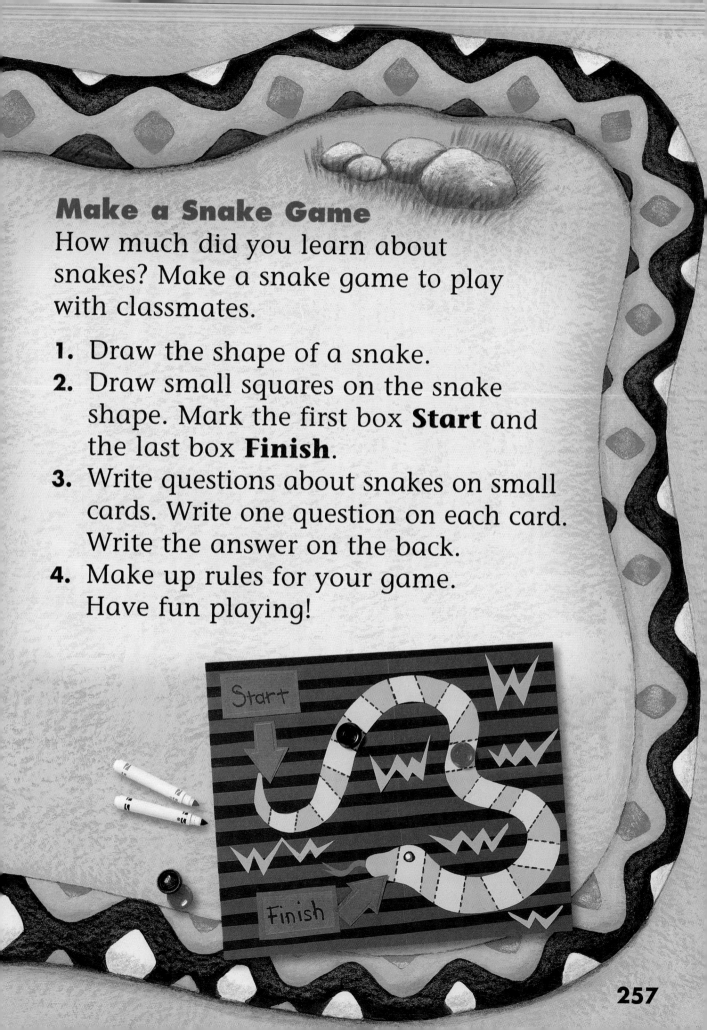

Make a Snake Game

How much did you learn about snakes? Make a snake game to play with classmates.

1. Draw the shape of a snake.
2. Draw small squares on the snake shape. Mark the first box **Start** and the last box **Finish**.
3. Write questions about snakes on small cards. Write one question on each card. Write the answer on the back.
4. Make up rules for your game. Have fun playing!

Plural Nouns That Change Spelling

A **plural noun** names more than one person, place, animal, or thing.

Some nouns change spelling to name more than one.

The **leaf** fell from the tree.

The snakes hide in the **leaves.**

Singular Nouns	Plural Nouns
goose	geese
foot	feet
tooth	teeth
wolf	wolves
leaf	leaves
mouse	mice

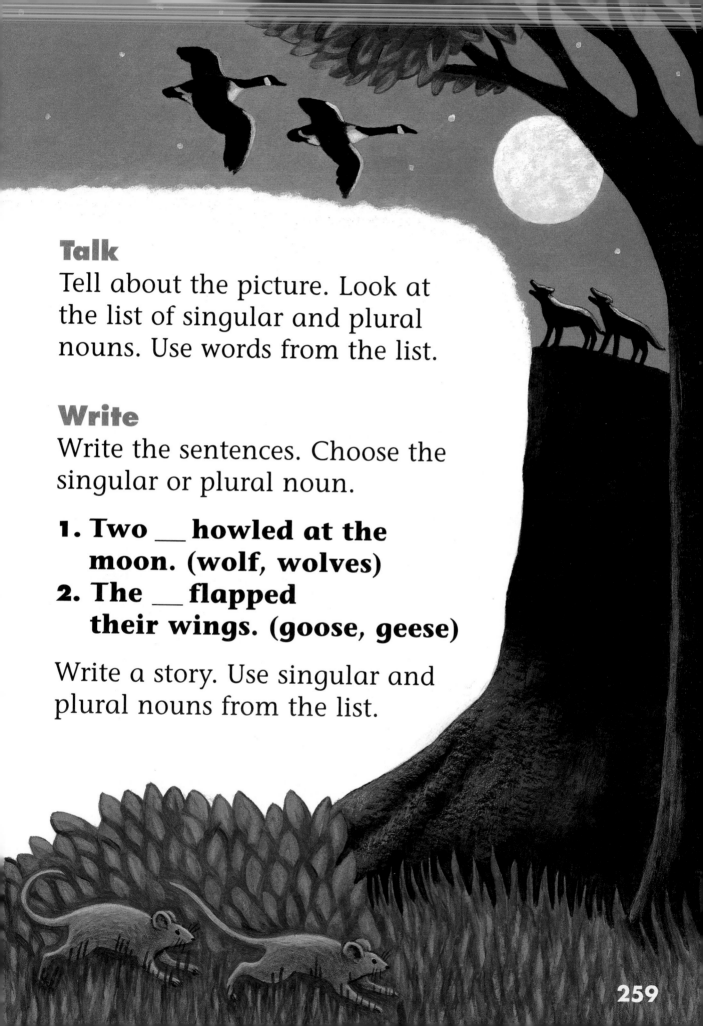

Talk

Tell about the picture. Look at the list of singular and plural nouns. Use words from the list.

Write

Write the sentences. Choose the singular or plural noun.

1. **Two __ howled at the moon. (wolf, wolves)**
2. **The __ flapped their wings. (goose, geese)**

Write a story. Use singular and plural nouns from the list.

Spiders Up Close

by Judy Nayer

jumping spider

spider crab

marbled orb weaver

Have You Heard?

There are 30,000 different kinds of spiders!

The world is full of spiders. Spiders have been on Earth since before the first dinosaurs.

burrowing wolf spider

grass spider

water spider

You can find spiders in almost every place! They live on the ground, in trees, and under rocks. They live in sand and in water. They live in people's gardens, and even in people's houses!

Have You Heard?
Spiders can help us because they eat insects that harm our gardens.

Spiders' bodies range in size. Some are as small as the period at the end of this sentence. Some are large enough to cover this page!

tarantula

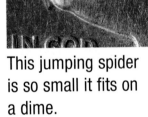

This jumping spider is so small it fits on a dime.

Have You Heard?

The biggest spider is huge—big enough to eat a mouse!

The female black widow (left) is much larger than the male (right).

The lynx spider is not an insect.

Some people call a spider an insect. But spiders are not insects. Can you tell the difference? Notice that the spider has eight legs. Insects have only six legs. Do not call a spider an insect!

The assassin bug (top) and the June bug (bottom) are insects.

Have You Heard?

Spiders use the hairs on their legs to sense what is around them.

A crab spider's body has two main parts.

How else can you tell the difference between a spider and an insect? Take a close look. A spider's body has two main parts. An insect's body has three main parts.

An ant's body has three main parts.

Have You Heard?

Many insects have wings.
Spiders never do.

Some spiders trap insects in a web. A spider's web is made of silk that comes from the spider's own body. Once a spider spins a web, it waits until an insect lands in the web.

This spider moves its web as a warning signal.

A grass spider sits on a wet web.

The orb spider spins a beautiful web.

Some spiders hunt insects the way cats hunt mice. They chase after insects until they can pounce on them.

A wolf spider attacks a cricket.

Have You Heard?

A jumping spider can make a leap forty times longer than its body.

A jumping spider begins its leap.

spider in a funnel web

lynx spider

arrow-shaped spider

golden web spider

trapdoor spider

black widow spider

The world is full of spiders. The next time you see one, take a close look. What you see may surprise you.

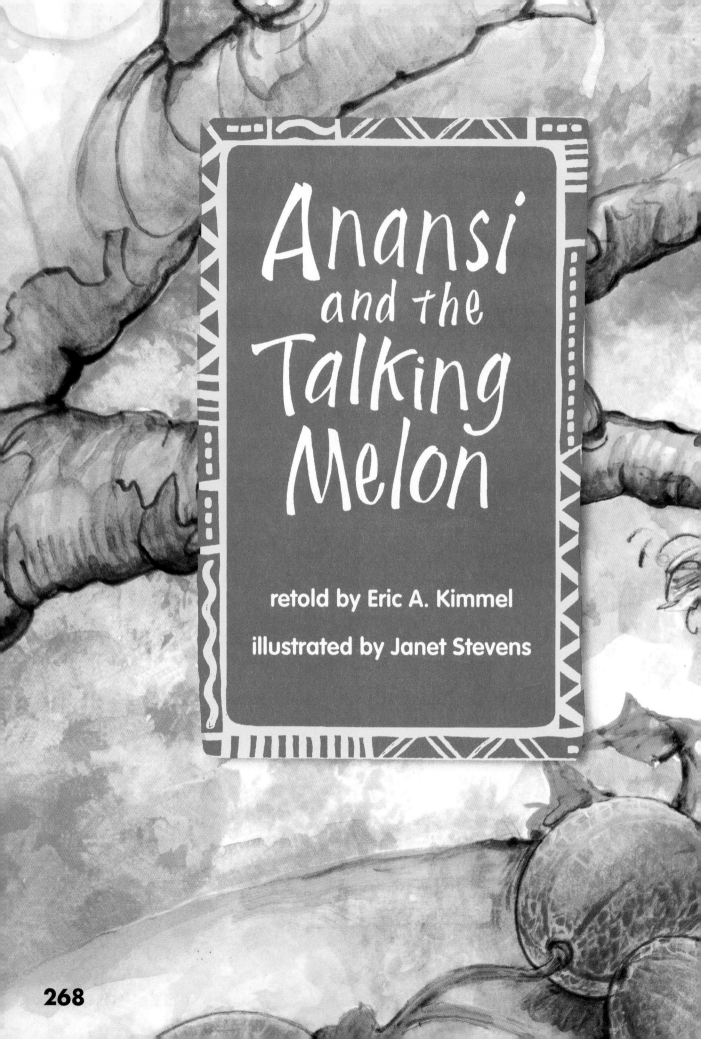

Anansi
and the
Talking
Melon

retold by Eric A. Kimmel

illustrated by Janet Stevens

One fine morning Anansi the Spider sat high up in a thorn tree looking down into Elephant's garden. Elephant was hoeing his melon patch. The ripe melons seemed to call out to Anansi, "Look how juicy and sweet we are! Come eat us!"

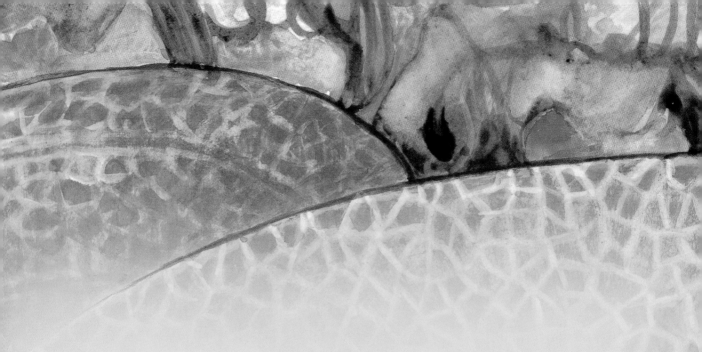

Anansi loved to eat melons, but he was much too lazy to grow them himself. So he sat up in the thorn tree, watching and waiting, while the sun rose high in the sky and the day grew warm. By the time noon came, it was too hot to work. Elephant put down his hoe and went inside his house to take a nap.

Here was the moment Anansi had been waiting for. He broke off a thorn and dropped down into the melon patch. He used the thorn to bore a hole in the biggest, ripest melon.

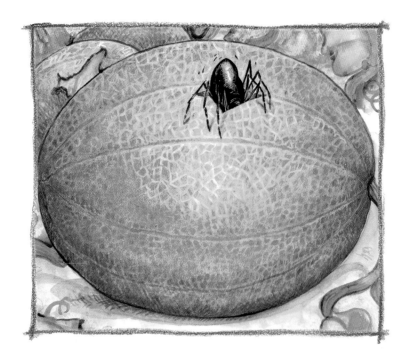

Anansi squeezed inside and started eating. He ate and ate until he was as round as a berry.

"I'm full," Anansi said at last. "Elephant will be coming back soon. It is time to go."

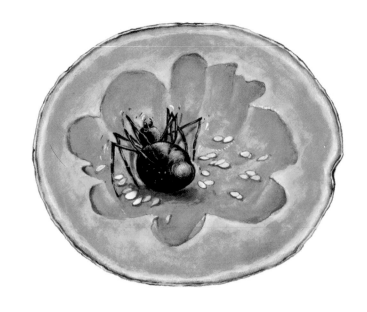

But when he tried to squeeze through the
hole, Anansi had a surprise. He didn't fit!
The hole was big enough for a thin spider,
but much too small for a fat one.

"I'm stuck!" Anansi cried. "I can't get out.
I will have to wait until I am thin again."

Anansi sat down
on a pile of melon
seeds and waited
to get thin. Time
passed slowly.

"I'm bored,"
Anansi said. "I wish
I had something to do."

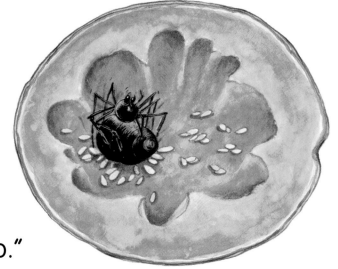

Just then he heard Elephant returning to the garden. Anansi had an idea. "When Elephant gets closer, I will say something. Elephant will think the melon is talking. What fun!"

Elephant walked over to the melon patch.
"Look at this fine melon. How big and ripe it
is!" he said, picking it up.

"Ouch!" cried Anansi.
Elephant jumped.
"Aah! Who said that?"

"I did. The melon," Anansi said.

"I didn't know melons could talk," said Elephant.

"Of course we do. We talk all the time. The trouble is, you never listen."

"I can't believe my ears!" Elephant exclaimed. "A talking melon! Who could believe it? I must show this to the king."

Elephant ran down the road, carrying the melon with Anansi inside. Along the way, he ran into Hippo.

"Where are you going with that melon?" Hippo asked.

"I'm taking it to the king," Elephant told him.

"What for? The king has hundreds of melons."

"He doesn't have one like this," Elephant
said. "This is a talking melon."

Hippo didn't believe Elephant. "A talking
melon? What an idea! That's as ridiculous as . . ."

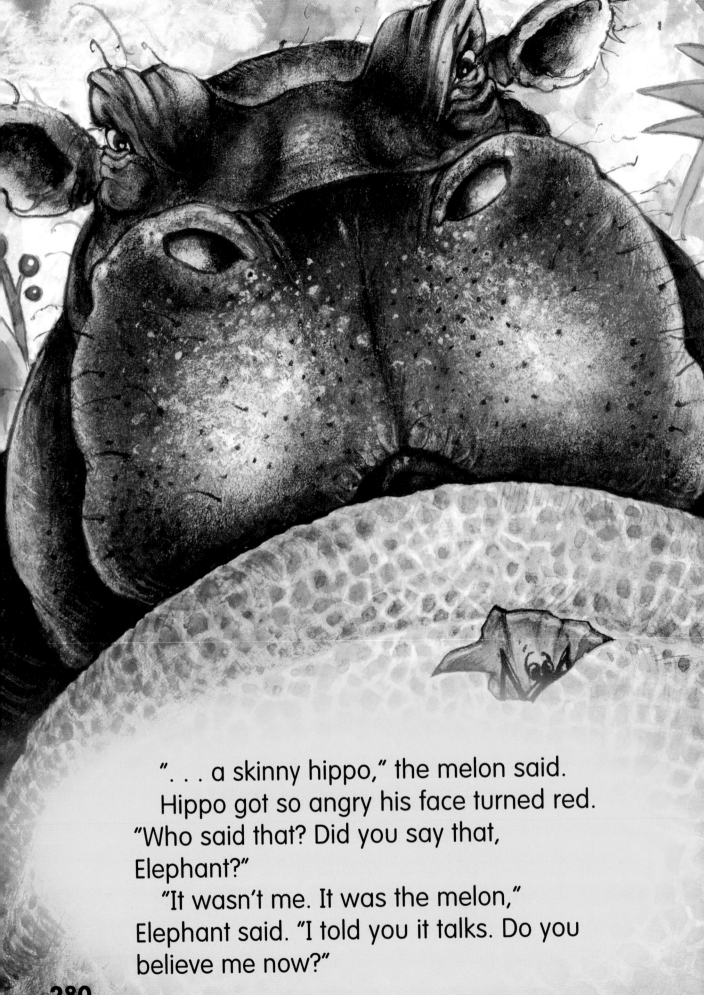

". . . a skinny hippo," the melon said.

Hippo got so angry his face turned red.
"Who said that? Did you say that,
Elephant?"

"It wasn't me. It was the melon,"
Elephant said. "I told you it talks. Do you
believe me now?"

"I do!" Hippo exclaimed. "I want to go with you. I want to hear what the king says when you show him this talking melon."

"Come along, then," said Elephant. So Elephant and Hippo went down the road together, carrying the melon.

By and by, they ran into Warthog. "Where are you taking that melon?" Warthog asked them.

"We're taking it to the king," Elephant and Hippo told him.

"What for? The king has hundreds of melons," Warthog said.

"He doesn't have one like this," Hippo replied. "This melon talks. I heard it."

Warthog started to laugh. "A talking melon? Why, that's as ridiculous as . . ."

". . . a handsome warthog," said the melon.
Warthog got so angry he shook all over.
"Who said that? Did you say that, Elephant?
Did you say that, Hippo?"

"Of course not!" Hippo and Elephant told
him. "The melon talks. Do you believe us now?"

"I do!" cried Warthog. "Let me go with you. I want to see what the king does when you show him this talking melon."

So Warthog, Elephant, and Hippo went down the road together, carrying the melon.

Along the way, they met Ostrich, Rhino, and Turtle. They didn't believe the melon could talk either until they heard it for themselves. Then they wanted to come along too.

The animals came before the king. Elephant bowed low as he placed the melon at the king's feet.

The king looked down. "Why did you bring me a melon?" he asked Elephant. "I have hundreds of melons growing in my garden."

"You don't have one like this," Elephant said. "This melon talks."

"A talking melon? I don't believe it. Say something, Melon." The king prodded the melon with his foot.

The melon said nothing.

"Melon," the king said in a slightly louder voice, "there is no reason to be shy. Say whatever you like. I only want to hear you talk."

The melon still said nothing. The king grew impatient.

"Melon, if you can talk, I want you to say something. I command you to speak."

The melon did not make a sound.

The king gave up. "Oh, this is a stupid melon!" he said.

Just then the melon spoke. "Stupid, am I? Why do you say that? I'm not the one who talks to melons!"

The animals had never seen the king so angry. "How dare this melon insult me!" he shouted. The king picked up the melon and hurled it as far as he could.

The melon bounced and rolled all the way to Elephant's house. *KPOM!* It smacked into the thorn tree and burst into pieces. Anansi picked himself up from among the bits of melon rind.

All the excitement had made him thin. And now that he was thin again, he was hungry. Anansi climbed the banana tree. He settled himself in the middle of a big bunch of bananas and started eating.

Elephant returned. He went straight to the melon patch.

"You melons got me in trouble with the king!" Elephant said. "From now on, you can talk all you like. I'm not going to listen to a word you say!"

"Good for you, Elephant!" Anansi called from the bananas. "We bananas should have warned you. Talking melons are nothing but trouble."

About the Author and the Illustrator

Eric A. Kimmel

Eric A. Kimmel is an author and a storyteller. He likes telling folktales. Mr. Kimmel likes stories that are fun and can teach something. "Kids are an excellent audience," he says.

Janet Stevens

"I have been drawing as long as I can remember," says Janet Stevens. Her family called her "the artist" when she was a child.

The animals she draws often wear sneakers and Hawaiian shirts!

Reader Response

Let's Talk
Would it be fun to be Anansi? Why or why not?

Let's Think
What do you think might happen next if the story kept going?

Test Prep
Let's Write
Pretend the animals meet for lunch after the story ends. Write what you think each animal will say about the talking melon.

Be a Mime

A mime tells a story without using words. Can you tell part of this story without words?

1. Choose a favorite part of the story.
2. Ask a classmate to read the words. Think of a way to act it out.
3. Practice your parts together.
4. Perform for your classmates.

Language Arts

Possessive Nouns

A noun that shows who or what owns something is a **possessive noun**. Add an apostrophe **'** and **-s** when the noun is singular.

Sentence: The web <u>of the spider</u> is sticky.

Write: The **spider's** web is sticky.

Add an apostrophe **'** after **-s** when the noun is plural.

Sentence: The father <u>of the girls</u> bought them a hand lens.

Write: The **girls'** father bought them a hand lens.

Talk

Talk about the picture. Describe the spider. Begin with the words: **The spider's . . .**

Write

Rewrite the sentences. Use **-'s** or **-s'** to show who or what owns something.

1. I looked at the body <u>of the spider</u>.

2. The legs <u>of the bugs</u> are stuck in the web.

Draw a picture of yourself and a friend. Label the picture with nouns. Then write sentences using possessive nouns.

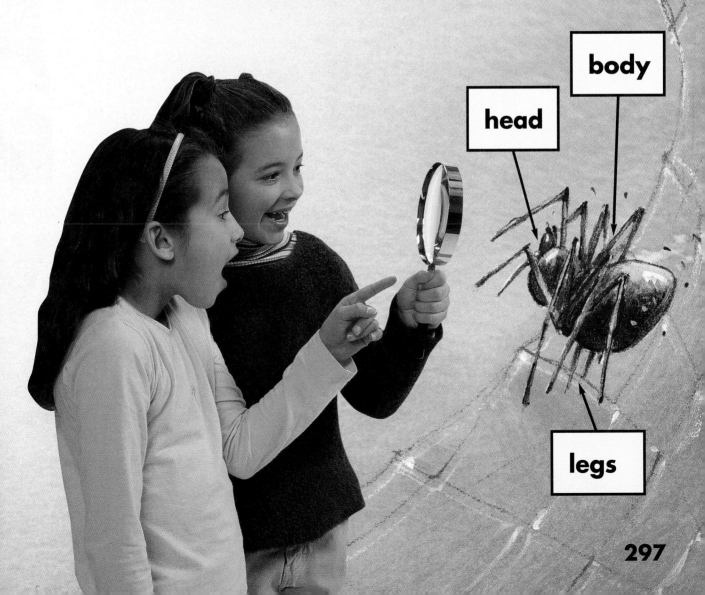

head

body

legs

Vocabulary Review

Words I Know

The Ugly Duckling

DUCK

beak
explore
keep
myself
paddle
surface
warm

Eye Spy

Seeing

brain
hidden
messages
mirror
thumb
whole

Furry Mouse

TWO MICE

another
bottle
cage
follow
food
wheel

The Old Gollywampus

Snakes

between

enemy

medicine

peels

scales

underneath

Spiders Up Close

Anansi and the Talking Melon

enough

exclaimed

patch

ripe

squeeze

until

Test Talk

Use a Chart

A test may have a question about a chart. Use what you see on the chart to answer the question.

A test about *Snakes* might show you the chart below and ask you a question.

1. Which snake is the longest?

(A) **Cobra**

(B) **Garter**

(C) **Python**

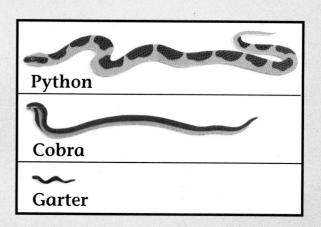

Python

Cobra

Garter

Think about what the question is asking. Then look at the chart for the answer.

Here is how one girl figured out her answer.

I see snakes on the chart. The chart shows me how long each snake is. I need to find out which snake is the longest. The answer is C.

Try it!

Use what you have learned to answer this test question about *Snakes*.

2. Look at the chart. Which snake is the shortest?

(A) **Python**

(B) **Garter**

(C) **Cobra**

Side by Side

How can we
learn and work
well together?

How I Beat The Giants

by Anne Phillips
illustrated by Jack Davis

My friends and I had a game against
the Giants. It turned out they really were
giants! Those players were as big as
trees.

"Don't worry," said Howie.
"We'll show those giants."
But after the Giants batted,
the score was a hundred to zero.
Things were beginning to look bad.

Now it was my turn at bat. I gripped
the bat and swung. Strike one! Strike
two! Strike three! I was out! Things were
getting worse.

Jamie's been our best batter since first grade. She hit the ball. She ran around the bases. It was a run! The Giants were still winning, but things were getting better.

A little later, the Giants had a
thousand. We had a thousand and one.
The Giants were batting. Now, if we
could get them out, we could win the
game.

"Watch out!" said Kim. I nodded.
I pitched the ball. *Crack!* The ball flew
through the clouds all the way to the
moon. Then it bounced back! Wow!

"I've got it!" I shouted. I caught the ball. Jamie caught me. Howie caught Jamie. Kim caught Howie.

The Giants were out! We had won!

So that's how I beat the Giants. . .
with a little help from my friends.

Play Ball

by Stephen Krensky

illustrated by Susanna Natti

Lionel and his friends were playing baseball.
Lionel was getting a lot of advice.

"Dive for those balls, Lionel,"
said Jeffrey, when a ball got past him.

"Catch with two hands," said Sarah,
when a ball jumped off his glove.

When Lionel came up to bat, Ellen
was pitching.
"Easy out," she said.

Lionel gripped the bat firmly.

He would show her how wrong she was.

Ellen made her windup.

The pitch sailed in.

Lionel waited—and then he swung hard.

The bat met the ball

with a sharp *Craaccck!*

The ball went up and up and up.

It sailed over a fence.

CRASH!

"That sounded like a window," said Max.

"At the Barries'," said Sarah.

Lionel froze. He squeezed his eyes shut.
This was going to be terrible.
Mr. Barrie was bound to yell at him.

His parents would find out.

They would yell too.

Lionel opened his eyes. Mr. Barrie

was approaching with a ball

in his hand.

"Who hit this ball?" he asked.

Lionel swallowed hard.

He didn't want anyone else

getting in trouble for his mistake.

"I did," he said.

"I hit it too," said Jeffrey behind him.

He had picked up his bat.

"And me," said Max,

his bat now resting on his shoulder.

"I got a piece of it," said George.

"Don't forget me," said Sarah.

"And us," said everyone else together.
They were all holding their bats.

Mr. Barrie looked around.
"I see," he said, trying to look serious.

"It was a real team effort."
He rubbed his chin.

"Well, since you all shared in the hit,
you can all help me fix the window later.
Fair enough?"

Everyone nodded.

Mr. Barrie returned to his house.

Lionel looked at everybody and sighed.
"Thanks," he said.

Jeffrey smiled. "It could have been any of us.
Besides," he added, "that's what friends are for."

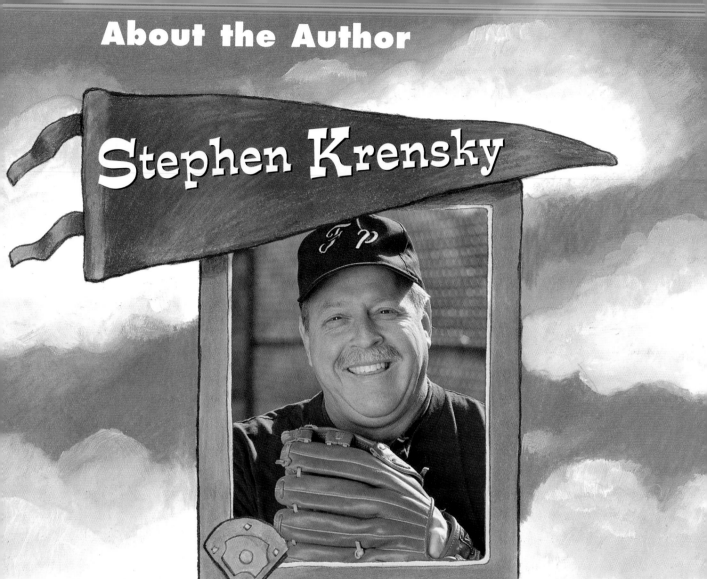

Stephen Krensky

Stephen Krensky says that when he writes for children, he writes "the kind of stories I like best." He has many interests. He writes about them in his books. He has written about ice cream, dinosaurs, treasure hunts, and trolls. He dedicated "Play Ball" to "all the friends on Eaton Road." That's where Mr. Krensky lives.

Reader Response

Let's Talk

What was the most exciting part of the story? Why did you like it?

Let's Think

What does Mr. Barrie mean when he says, "It was a real team effort"?

Test Prep
Let's Write

How will Lionel and his friends fix the broken window? Write what might happen next.

Tell the News

Pretend you are a reporter in front of a TV camera. Report what happened to Lionel and his friends.

1. Write about where, when, and how the window was broken.
2. Write about what happened after the window was broken.
3. Report your story to the class.

Language Arts

Verbs

A **verb** is a word that can show action.

The pitcher **throws** the ball.

The dog **barks** at the pitcher.

What does the person, animal, or thing do in each sentence?

noun	verb
pitcher	throws
dog	barks

Talk

Tell what the people, animals, and things are doing in the picture. Add nouns and verbs to the chart.

Write

Write the sentences. Underline the person, animal, or thing that is doing something. Circle each verb.

1. **The fans cheer their team.**
2. **The bat hit the ball.**

Write sentences of your own.
Circle the verbs in your sentences.

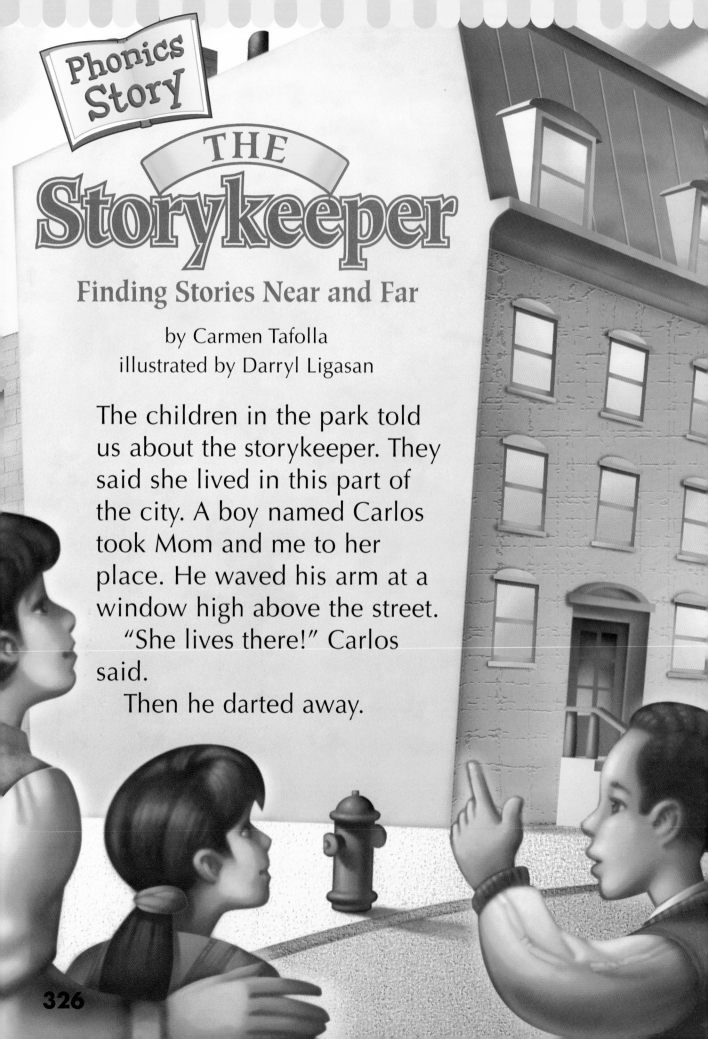

THE
Storykeeper

Finding Stories Near and Far

by Carmen Tafolla
illustrated by Darryl Ligasan

The children in the park told us about the storykeeper. They said she lived in this part of the city. A boy named Carlos took Mom and me to her place. He waved his arm at a window high above the street.

"She lives there!" Carlos said.

Then he darted away.

326

The storykeeper has dark hair and eyes as bright as stars. I liked her as soon as I met her. We sat in a large room. Here are my questions and her answers.

Q: Are you the storykeeper?

A: Yes! That is what the children call me.

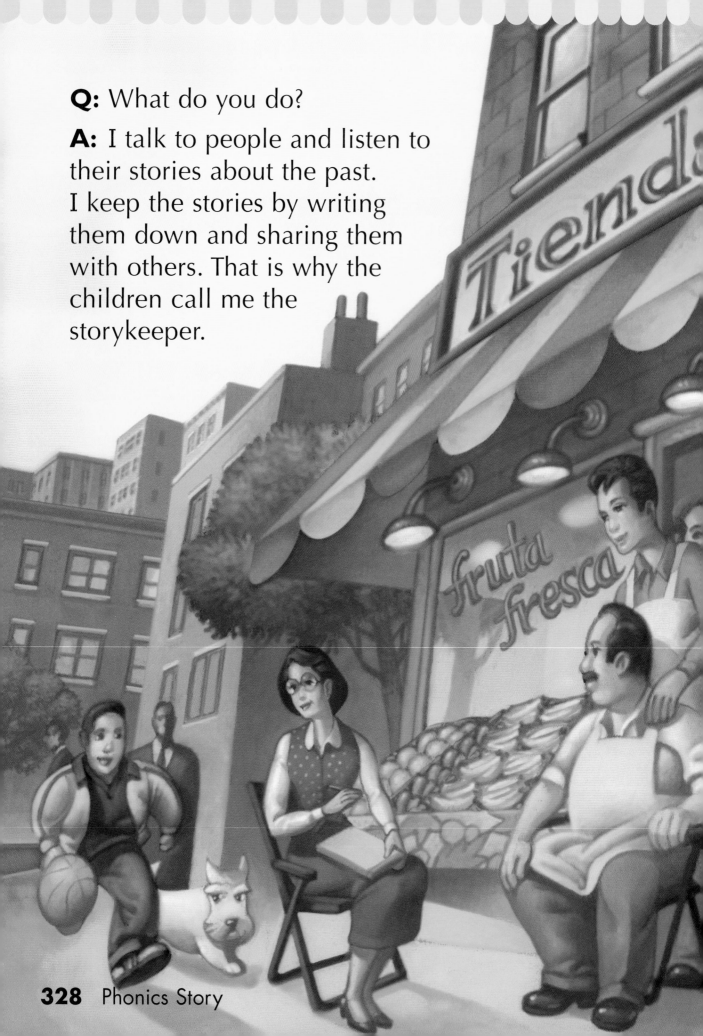

Q: What do you do?

A: I talk to people and listen to their stories about the past. I keep the stories by writing them down and sharing them with others. That is why the children call me the storykeeper.

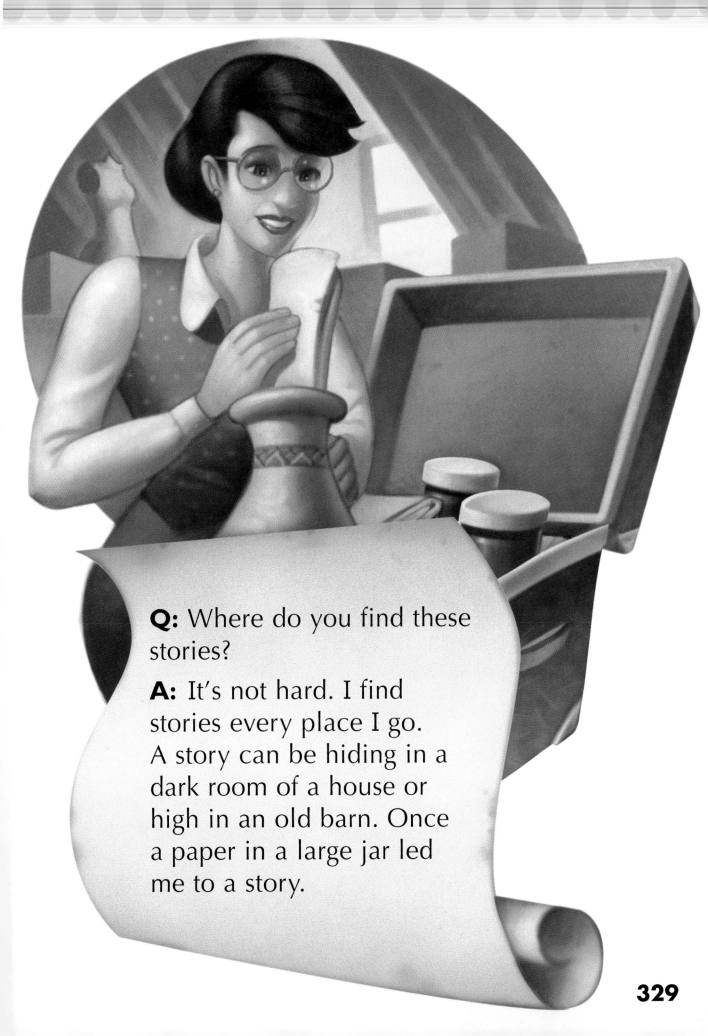

Q: Where do you find these stories?

A: It's not hard. I find stories every place I go. A story can be hiding in a dark room of a house or high in an old barn. Once a paper in a large jar led me to a story.

Q: Do you ever go far to find a story?

A: Sometimes I go to a city far away. I go many places to find stories. But most of the time I start here. In this city there are many stories.

Once I met a man with a guitar in the park. He told stories with his songs.

Q: Why are these stories so important?

A: I'm hoping that if we learn stories about each other, we can start to make the world a better place.

"Thank you," I said. "I can hardly wait to tell other children what you have shared with me."

"Good!" she said. "Then you will be a storykeeper too!"

People, People, Everywhere!

by Nancy Van Laan

illustrated by Nadine Bernard Westcott

People, people, everywhere!
Running here, running there!
People racing round the town,
Going up!
Going down!
People riding to the top.
Getting off!
Please press *STOP!*

People dashing round the park,
Walking dogs . . .
Bark! Bark! Bark!

People waiting in a line.
Here's the bus!
Just in time!

Catching taxis . . . catching trains . . .
Catching subways . . . catching planes.
Take a copter
Up! Up! Up!
Take a ferry,
Shlup! Shlup! Shlup!

People, people, everywhere!
Working here, working there.
Policemen walking city beats.
Vendors selling treats to eat.

338

SHOP

BREAD

Workers building buildings tall,
Way up high.
Watch out! Don't fall!

People working under town,
Digging, fixing, underground.
Tunneling subways, sealing leaks,
Way beneath the city streets.

Teachers teaching . . . plumbers plumbing . . .
Doctors doctoring . . . drummers drumming . . .

Here's a fire truck
Whizzing, wailing!
In the harbor,
Boats are sailing!

Children, children, everywhere!
Playing here, playing there.
In the alleys . . . at the park . . .
In the hallways after dark.
Jumping rope, playing ball,
Playing anything at all!
Riding bikes, tic-tac-toe,
Children shouting, "Go! Go! Go!"
Upstairs, downstairs,
Running round,
Children playing all through town!

People, people, everywhere!
Leaving here, going there.
Moving to a quiet place
In the country where there's space.
Room to work and room to play,
No more waiting every day.
No more traffic, no more noise,
Lots of space for lots of toys.

347

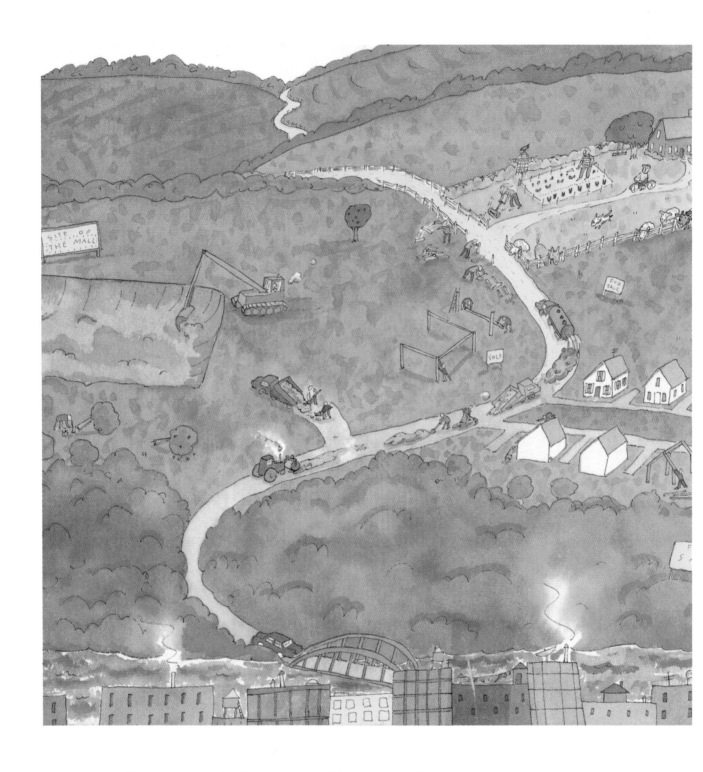

Trees and flowers all around,
A perfect place to build a town.

People here, people there,
People, people, everywhere!

About the Author
Nancy Van Laan

Nancy Van Laan has always liked to write. "When I was little, I would spend long afternoons writing poems, plays, and stories," she says.

Ms. Van Laan writes her stories by hand. "My pages are full of scribbles and cross-outs."

About the Illustrator
Nadine Bernard Westcott

Nadine Bernard Westcott first planned to become a teacher. Instead she became a very popular book illustrator.

Ms. Westcott remembers drawing as a child. She sketched on the back of paper place mats.

City Music

by Tony Mitton

Snap your fingers.
Tap your feet.
Step out a rhythm
down the street.

Rap on a litter bin.
Stamp on the ground.
City music
is all around.

Beep says motor-car.
Ding says bike.
City music
is what we like.

Reader Response

Let's Talk

Would you rather live in the city or in the country? Why?

Let's Think

What is happening to the country at the end of the story? How do you know?

Test Prep
Let's Write

Tell what is alike and different about living in the country and in the city. Write sentences about each place. Use the story and pictures to help you.

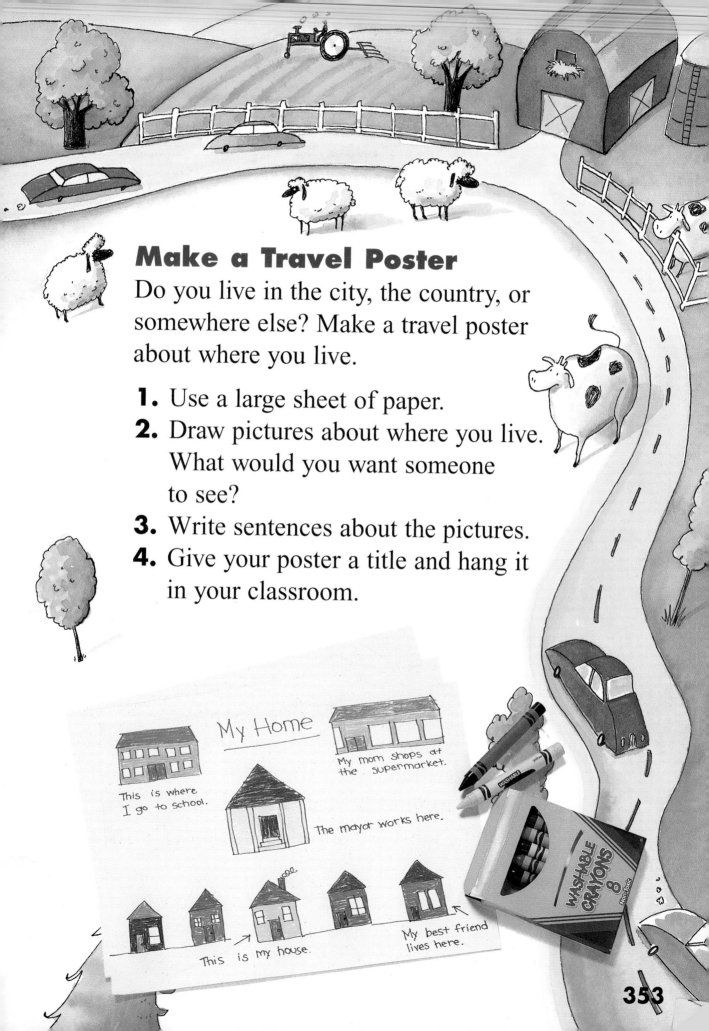

Make a Travel Poster

Do you live in the city, the country, or somewhere else? Make a travel poster about where you live.

1. Use a large sheet of paper.
2. Draw pictures about where you live. What would you want someone to see?
3. Write sentences about the pictures.
4. Give your poster a title and hang it in your classroom.

My Home

This is where I go to school.

My mom shops at the supermarket.

The mayor works here.

This is my house.

My best friend lives here.

353

Language Arts

Verbs with Singular Nouns and Plural Nouns

Verbs may tell what one, two, or more people, animals, or things do. Add **-s** to verbs that tell what one person, animal, or thing does. Do not add **-s** to verbs that tell about two or more.

The firefighter **climbs** the ladder.

The dogs **bark** at the cat.

climbs ── (**firefighter**) ── ── (**dogs**) ── bark

Talk

Tell what is happening in the picture. Think about what the firefighter and the dogs might do. Add verbs to the webs. Tell why each verb should have an **-s** or not.

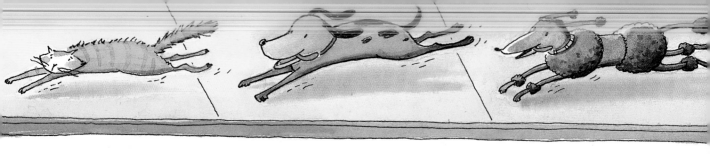

Write

Write the sentences. Choose the correct verb.

1. The dogs ___ the cat. (scare, scares)
2. The cat ___ in the tree. (sit, sits)

Write sentences about what is happening in the picture. Use the verbs in the box. Remember to add **-s** to verbs with a singular noun.

verbs
blow
call
run
climb
ride
bark
stop
drive
want

New
Best
Friends

by Judy Nayer

illustrated by
Bernard Adnet

Hal missed Uncle Lou. His uncle flew
home a few weeks ago.

"Why don't you write Uncle Lou a letter?"
said his mom. "He'd love to hear from you."

So Hal did. He used his computer.

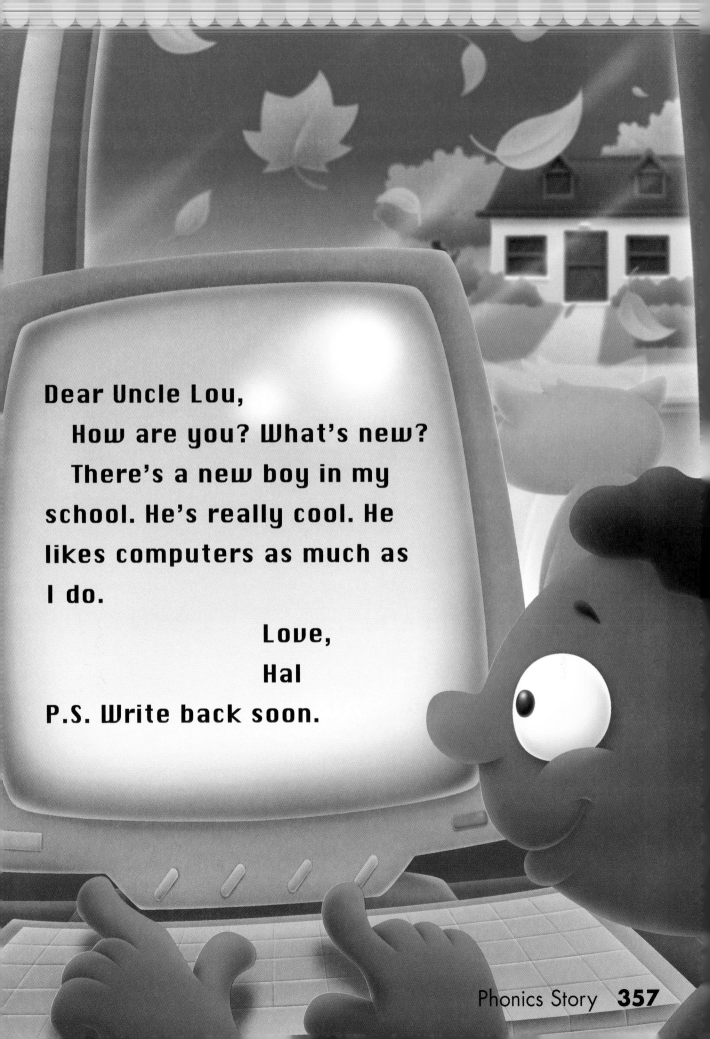

Dear Uncle Lou,
   How are you? What's new?
   There's a new boy in my
school. He's really cool. He
likes computers as much as
I do.

                    Love,
                    Hal

P.S. Write back soon.

A few days later, Hal wrote to Uncle Lou again.

Dear Uncle Lou,
   You're not going to believe it! The new boy lives across the street! We sometimes walk to school together.
                    Love,
                    Hal
P.S. His name is Luís!

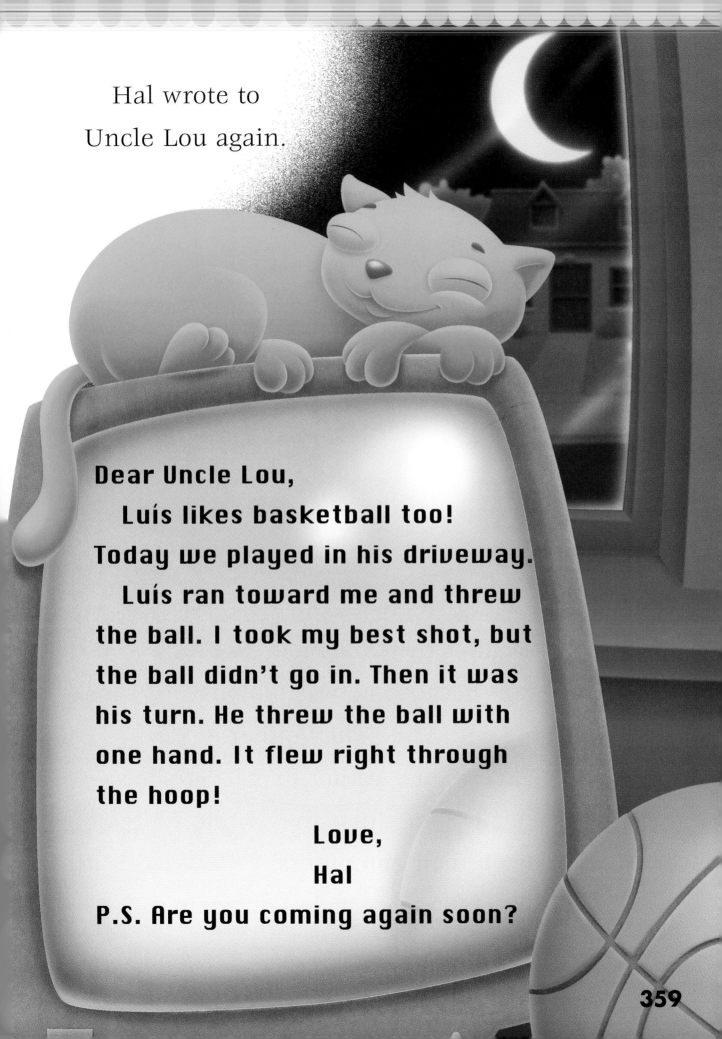

Hal wrote to
Uncle Lou again.

Dear Uncle Lou,
 Luís likes basketball too!
Today we played in his driveway.
 Luís ran toward me and threw
the ball. I took my best shot, but
the ball didn't go in. Then it was
his turn. He threw the ball with
one hand. It flew right through
the hoop!

                    Love,
                    Hal

P.S. Are you coming again soon?

Hal didn't write to Uncle Lou for a few days because he was too busy playing with Luís. They either played computer games or basketball. Sometimes they wrote stories on their computers.

Then Hal wrote Uncle Lou again.

Dear Uncle Lou,

 You've got to see the room Luís has. We either play with his computer or with his other cool space stuff. We even learned about the crew that flew to the moon. Zoom! Zoom!

Love,
Hal

P.S. Luís says I'm his best friend. Isn't that cool?

The next day Hal got a
letter from Uncle Lou. Hal
read it on his computer.

Dear Hal,
   I'm coming to town next
week. I can stay a few
days. I'd like to meet your
new friend.
                    Love,
                    Uncle Lou

Uncle Lou arrived on Tuesday
afternoon.

He and Hal's new best friend, Luís,
got along just fine.

WANTED: BEST FRIEND

by A. M. Monson
illustrated by Lynn Munsinger

Cat and Mouse sat at the table. They were playing checkers. The two played the game so often that Cat sometimes made up new rules.

"That's it," said Cat. "I won." He set up the checkers for another game.

"That's the third time you've won," complained Mouse. "Let's play crazy eights now."

"I hate crazy eights," said Cat. "You take forever to decide which card to play."

"But when we play crazy eights, I win sometimes," said Mouse. He folded his arms across his chest. "Either we play crazy eights or I go home."

"All right," said Cat. "Go home. I'll find someone else to play with me."

"Fine," said Mouse. He picked up his hat and left.

Cat scratched his head. How would he find
another friend? Suddenly he had an idea.
He grabbed a piece of paper and a pencil.
He wrote:

WANTED: BEST FRIEND
MUST LIKE TO PLAY GAMES
SEE CAT *IMMEDIATELY!*

Then he called *The Hollow Log Gazette.*

Two days later there was a knock at Cat's door.
"Did you advertise for a friend?" asked Mole.
"Yes," answered Cat. "Come in." He hoped Mole
liked to play checkers as much as he did.

"How about some munchies?" asked Mole.

"Help yourself," said Cat.

Mole disappeared into the kitchen.

When he came out, he was carrying a can of soda, a jar of peanut butter, crackers, bananas, an ice cream bar, and a bag of pretzels. The can of soda tumbled to the floor. Mole kicked it toward the table.

"Ah-h," said Mole. He tossed the banana peel over his shoulder. "Now I'm ready to play."

Cat moved his checker first. Mole stuffed his mouth with crackers and peanut butter.

"Your turn," said Cat.

Mole dumped all the pretzels onto the table, then moved his playing piece.

Cat smiled. He jumped over Mole's checker using his own. "Oh, dear," said Cat. His finger sank into a gooey glob of peanut butter when he touched Mole's checker.

"Time for a drink," said Mole. "No, wait!" said Cat. But he was too late. Orange soda sprayed from the can into Cat's face.

"This will not do," said Cat. He raced for a towel. "You cannot be a slob and be my best friend."

Cat avoided Mole's sticky fingers and led him by the arm out of the house.

He'd just finished cleaning up Mole's mess
when he heard another knock at the door.

"Did you advertise for a friend?" asked Otter.
He carried a large and bumpy duffel bag.
"Yes, I did," said Cat. "Come in."

"I have everything we need to have fun," said Otter. He unzipped the bag. "Baseball, basketball, softball, football, soccer ball . . ."

"But I like to play checkers," said Cat. Balls bounced around his feet.

"B-or-ring!" said Otter. "These games are a lot more fun. Watch." He grabbed the basketball and tossed it into a lamp shade.

"Two points!" he yelled.

Cat raced to steady the wobbling lamp.
A football sailed past his head and through
the rabbit ears on the television.

"Touchdown!" cheered Otter.

"No more," said Cat. But he was too late.
Otter kicked the soccer ball into the fireplace.

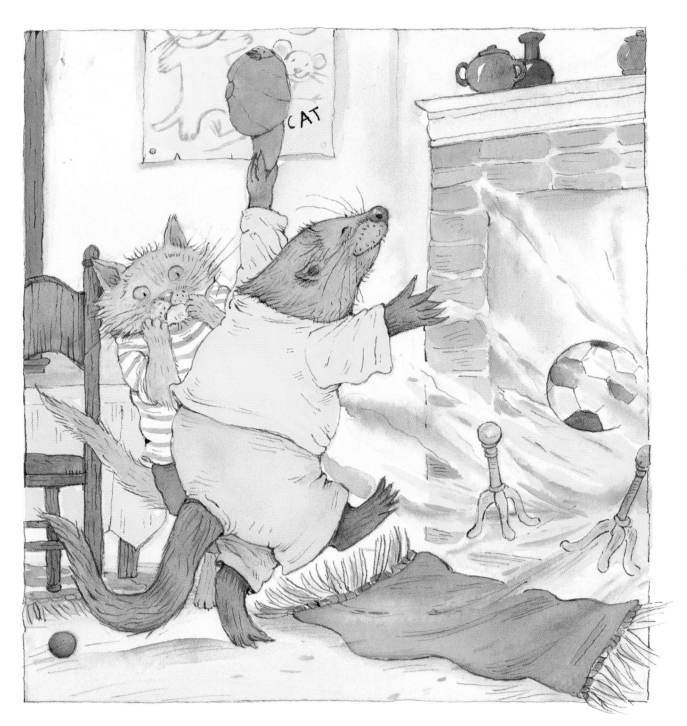

"Goal!" cried Otter.

"This will not do," said Cat.
He stamped out sparks. "You cannot burn my house down and be my best friend."

He made Otter pick up all the balls, then showed him to the door.

He plopped into his big stuffed chair. "If Mouse had a phone, I would call and invite him back." Suddenly he had an idea. He grabbed a piece of paper and a pencil. He wrote:

MOUSE,
PLEASE COME BACK.
WILLING TO PLAY CRAZY EIGHTS.
CAT

Then he called *The Hollow Log Gazette.*
Two days later there was a knock at Cat's door.

"Mouse," said Cat. "I'm so happy to see you."
He led his friend to the table.

"I'm thirsty," said Mouse. He disappeared into
the kitchen, then returned with a glass of water.

Cat watched Mouse set the glass on a napkin. "You're so tidy," said Cat.

"Thank you," said Mouse.

"And you never throw things around my house," said Cat.

"I wouldn't dream of it," said Mouse.

Cat smiled. "Mouse," he said, "you're my kind of best friend."

And the two of them began to play crazy eights.

About the Author and the Illustrator

A. M. Monson

A. M. Monson went to a one-room school in Wisconsin. She is an animal lover and enjoys nature.

Ms. Monson now lives in Minnesota. She likes to cross-country ski and camp.

Lynn Munsinger

Lynn Munsinger is the illustrator of over forty children's books. She is well known for her drawings of Tacky the Penguin.

Ms. Munsinger lives in New York City with her two dogs. She likes to ski and travel.

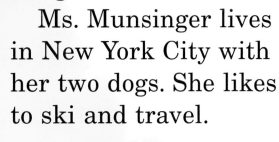

Reader Response

Let's Talk

Would you want Cat for a friend? Why or why not?

Let's Think

Why does Cat decide to play Crazy Eights with Mouse at the end of the story?

Test Prep
Let's Write

Cat wants Mouse to come back. Pretend you are Cat. Write a letter to Mouse. Tell why you want Mouse to come back. Find reasons in the story.

Make a Wanted Poster for a New Friend

What do you like about your friends? Make a wanted poster for a new friend.

1. Use a large sheet of paper.
2. Write three things that tell what you want your friend to be like.
3. Draw pictures to go with what you wrote.
4. Hang your poster in the classroom for others to see.

WANTED
A New Friend
① I want my friend to be nice.
② I want my friend to be funny.
③ I want my friend to like riding a bike.

Verb Tenses

Verbs can tell about action that is taking place in the past, in the present, or in the future.

The girl **mixed** the glue yesterday.

The boy and girl **paint** the piñata today.

The children **will hang** the piñata tomorrow.

past	present	future
mixed	paint	will hang

Talk

The children are getting ready for a party. Talk about what the children did yesterday. What do they do now? What will they do tomorrow? Tell where each verb belongs on the chart.

Write

Write these sentences.
Choose the correct verb tense.

1. The girl ___ the bowl yesterday.
   (wash, washed, will wash)
2. The children ___ the brushes now.
   (wash, washed, will wash)
3. Who ___ the dishes tomorrow?
   (wash, washed, will wash)

Pretend you are at a school picnic. Write
sentences. Use past, present, and future verbs.

Four Clues for Chee

by Juanita Havill • illustrated by Donna Perrone

Grandfather was standing next to the door. Chee hurried over to him.

"What are you doing, Grandfather?" Chee asked.

"I'm making something for you, Chee," said Grandfather. "But it is a surprise."

Then Grandfather said, "I will give you four clues. My surprise comes from a tree. There is nothing in it, but something pours out of it. It can sound like a bird or an echo in a canyon."

Next, he gave Chee one more clue. "Breath and fingers bring its sound to us."

Chee tried to think about Grandfather's four clues. He brought home a book and read all about trees. He learned that paper comes from trees.

Maybe Grandfather is drawing a picture. But how can a picture have nothing in it?

Chee's mother brought food home from the store. Chee carried the boxes to the kitchen for her. A box can be empty, he thought. A box can come from a tree.

Next, Chee thought about the third clue. A box can't sound like a bird. He tried shouting in the box. A box doesn't sound like a bird or a canyon.

Chee cried out his name to the canyon. "Chee! Chee! Chee!" the canyon sang. Then he knew.

"With your gift I will make sounds," Chee said to Grandfather. "I will use my breath and my fingers."

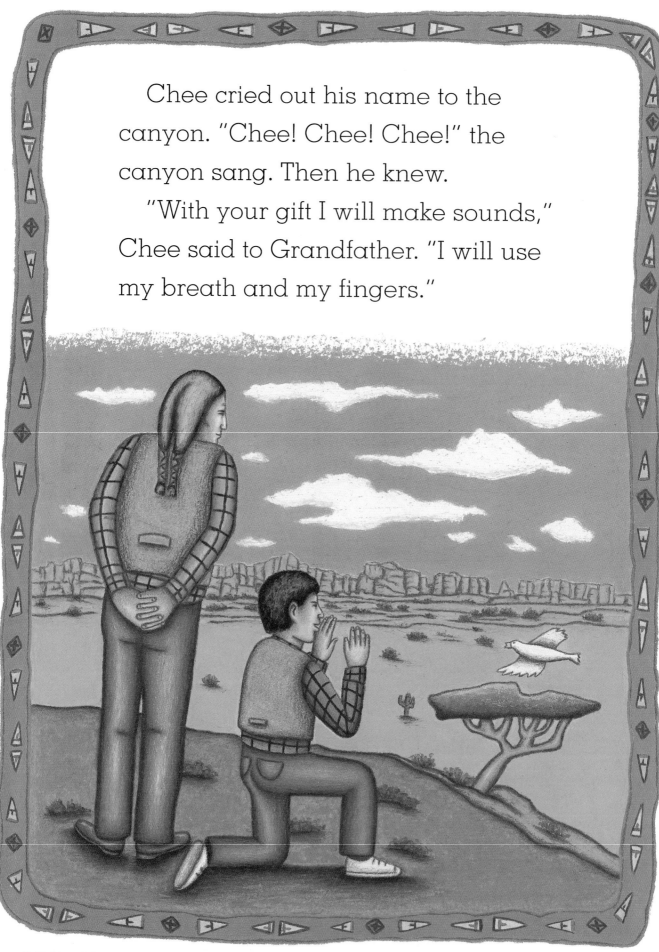

With Grandfather's gift, Chee made
sounds. With his breath and fingers,
he made sounds. Now, beautiful
sounds pour from Chee's flute!

Young Cam Jansen
and the Dinosaur Game

by David A. Adler

illustrated by Susanna Natti

CONTENTS

1. I'm Going! I'm Going!

Honk! Honk!

"I'm going! I'm going!" Mr. Jansen said. He was driving his daughter Cam and her friend Eric Shelton to a birthday party.

Mr. Jansen stopped at the corner. He looked at the street signs. Then he said, "I'm sorry. I forgot where the party is. And I forgot to bring the invitation."

Honk! Honk!

"I'm going! I'm going!" Mr. Jansen said as he drove on. "But I don't know *where* I'm going."

Mr. Jansen drove to the next corner and parked the car.

Eric said, "I'm sure Cam remembers where the party is."

Cam closed her eyes and said, "Click!" Cam always closes her eyes and says "Click!" when she wants to remember something.

Cam has an amazing memory. "My memory is like a camera," she says. "I have a picture in my head of everything I've seen. 'Click!' is the sound my camera makes."

Cam's real name is Jennifer. But because of her great memory, people started to call her "the Camera." Then "the Camera" became just Cam.

"I'm looking at the invitation," Cam said, with her eyes closed. "It says, 'Come to a party for Jane Bell. 3:00 P.M., 86 Robin Lane.'"

Cam opened her eyes.

Mr. Jansen drove to 86 Robin Lane. There were balloons and a big HAPPY BIRTHDAY sign on the front door.

Mr. Bell opened the door and said, "Come in. Come in." He pointed to a big jar. "Before you join the others, guess how many dinosaurs are in this jar. Remember your guess. The best one wins the dinosaurs."

The jar was filled with blue, green, yellow, and red toy dinosaurs. Next to the jar were slips of paper, a few pens, and a shoe box.

Cam tried to count the dinosaurs. But she couldn't. Lots of dinosaurs were hidden behind other dinosaurs.

Cam wrote her guess on a slip of paper. She put the paper in the shoe box.

Eric looked at the jar. He looked for a long time. Then he wrote his guess on a slip of paper too. He put the paper in the shoe box. Eric said, "I hope I win."

Then Cam and Eric went to the kitchen. Their friends were there, sitting around the table.

2. The Dinosaur Game

Mrs. Bell said, "Good, everyone is here. I'll get the birthday cake." She carried a large cake to the table. The cake was covered with chocolate icing. Mrs. Bell lit the candles. Everyone sang "Happy Birthday." Then Mrs. Bell gave each child a piece of birthday cake.

They were all eating cake when Mr. Bell walked into the room. "I counted the dinosaurs," he said.

"There were 154 in the jar." Mr. Bell took a large piece of birthday cake.

Eric said, "I guessed 150. Maybe I'll win."

Rachel said, "I guessed 300."

"Who won?" Jane asked. "Who won the dinosaur game?"

Mr. Bell smiled. "We'll see," he said, "as soon as I finish eating."

Some children took a second piece of cake. Some went into the den to play.

When Mr. Bell finished, he brought in the shoe box. He turned it over and picked up a slip of paper. "180," he read. Then he showed it to everyone.

"That was my guess," Jane said.

One by one Mr. Bell read the guesses. "100 . . . 300 . . . 1,000 . . . 450 . . . 200."

Cam said, "200 was my guess."

Mr. Bell looked at the next slip of paper. He read, "150."

"That was my guess," Eric said.

Then Mr. Bell held up the last slip of paper and read, "154."

"That's mine," Robert said. "I win."

"You *do* win," Mr. Bell said. "You guessed the exact number. And here's your prize." He gave Robert the jar of dinosaurs.

Cam looked at Robert. Then she looked at the slip of paper in Mr. Bell's hand and said, "Click!"

Eric whispered to Cam, "That's amazing. He guessed the exact number of dinosaurs."

"Yes," Cam said. "It is amazing. It's almost *too* amazing."

3. Click!

Robert spilled the dinosaurs onto the table.

"They're cute," Rachel said.

"Can I have one?" Jason asked.

Rachel asked, "Can I have one too?"

"I'm not giving them away," Robert said. "I'm selling them."

"I want a red one," Rachel said. "I'll give you the money at school tomorrow."

"I want three green dinosaurs and two yellows," Jason said.

Mrs. Bell said, "Let's play another guessing game." She held up a small box. "I have something in here. It has a face and it runs. What is it?"

"Does it run fast?" Rachel asked.

Mrs. Bell said, "I hope not."

Eric asked, "Does it have eight legs? Is it a spider?"

Mrs. Bell said, "It doesn't have any legs."

Cam asked, "Does it have hands? Is it a watch?"

Cam was right.

Mr. Bell said, "Now let's play musical chairs." He set six chairs in a line. He turned on some music.

Then Mr. Bell told the children, "Walk around the chairs. When the music stops, sit down. Whoever can't find a seat is out of the game."

The children walked around the chairs. But not Cam. She looked at the chairs. She counted them. Then she closed her eyes and said, "Click!"

4. You Made Me Lose

The music stopped. Everyone but Cam sat down. She was out of the game. Mr. Bell took one chair away and turned on the music again.

Cam opened her eyes. She went over to the table. She looked at the slips of paper. Then, as Eric walked past, she whispered to him, "I have something to show you."

Eric turned, and the music stopped. Everyone but Eric sat down. He was out of the game. Mr. Bell took one chair away and turned on the music again.

When Robert walked past, Cam whispered to him, "And I have something to show you."

Robert turned, and the music stopped. Everyone but Robert sat down. Robert was out of the game. He told Cam, "You made me lose at musical chairs."

Cam said, "And I'll make you lose the dinosaurs too."

5. I'm Sharing

Cam said to Robert, "You wrote 154 *after* Jane's father counted the dinosaurs."

"I did not!" Robert said.

Cam told him, "Mr. Bell turned over the shoe box. The papers fell out upside down. They fell out in the same order they were put in.

"Jane's guess was first. Eric and I were the last to come to the party. Our guesses should have been last. But yours was."

Robert said, "Maybe the papers got mixed up."

Cam told him, "There were eight guesses but only seven kids are at the party. You guessed twice. You guessed when you came to the party. You guessed again after Jane's father told us there were 154 dinosaurs in the jar."

"I did not," Robert said.

Cam picked up Robert's winning guess. "And look at this," she said.

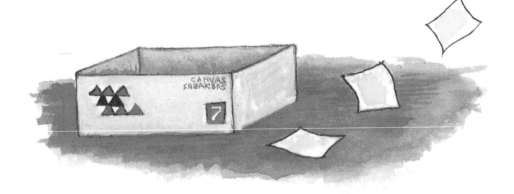

Cam pointed to a chocolate smudge. "You wrote this after we had birthday cake. That's why there's chocolate on it."

Cam and Eric looked at Robert's hands. There was chocolate on them too.

Robert looked down. "You're right," he said softly. "My real guess was 1,000 dinosaurs."

Robert put the dinosaurs back in the jar.

After the game of musical chairs ended, Robert talked to Mrs. Bell. He told her that Eric had really won the dinosaur game.

Mrs. Bell gave the jar to Eric.

Rachel said, "I want to buy a red dinosaur."

Jason said, "I want three green dinosaurs and two yellows."

Eric told them, "I'm not selling the dinosaurs. I'm sharing them."

The children sat in a circle. Eric walked around them. "One for you," he said as he gave each child a dinosaur. "And one for you. And one for you."

After Eric had given everyone else a dinosaur, he put one on an empty chair and said, "And one for me."

Eric walked around the circle again and again. He walked around until the big jar of toy dinosaurs was empty.

About the Author
David A. Adler

David A. Adler always liked to tell stories. When he was young, he made up stories to tell his brothers and sisters. Now Mr. Adler writes for children. "I feel very fortunate. I love writing, and it's so exciting for me to know that children enjoy reading what I have written."

"I have real fun with the Cam Jansen books," Mr. Adler says. "She is a delightful character."

About the Illustrator
Susanna Natti

Susanna Natti loves to read and draw. She likes to visit schools and talk about her artwork. Ms. Natti has illustrated all the Cam Jansen books as well as the Lionel books, written by Stephen Krensky.

Sharing

by Shel Silverstein

I'll share your toys, I'll share your money,
I'll share your toast, I'll share your honey,
I'll share your milk and your cookies too—
The hard part's sharing mine with you.

Reader Response

Let's Talk

Did the story keep you interested? Why or why not?

Let's Think

Why does Eric decide to share his dinosaurs at the end of the story?

Test Prep
Let's Write

Write your own mystery story. Make sure it has a beginning, middle, and end.

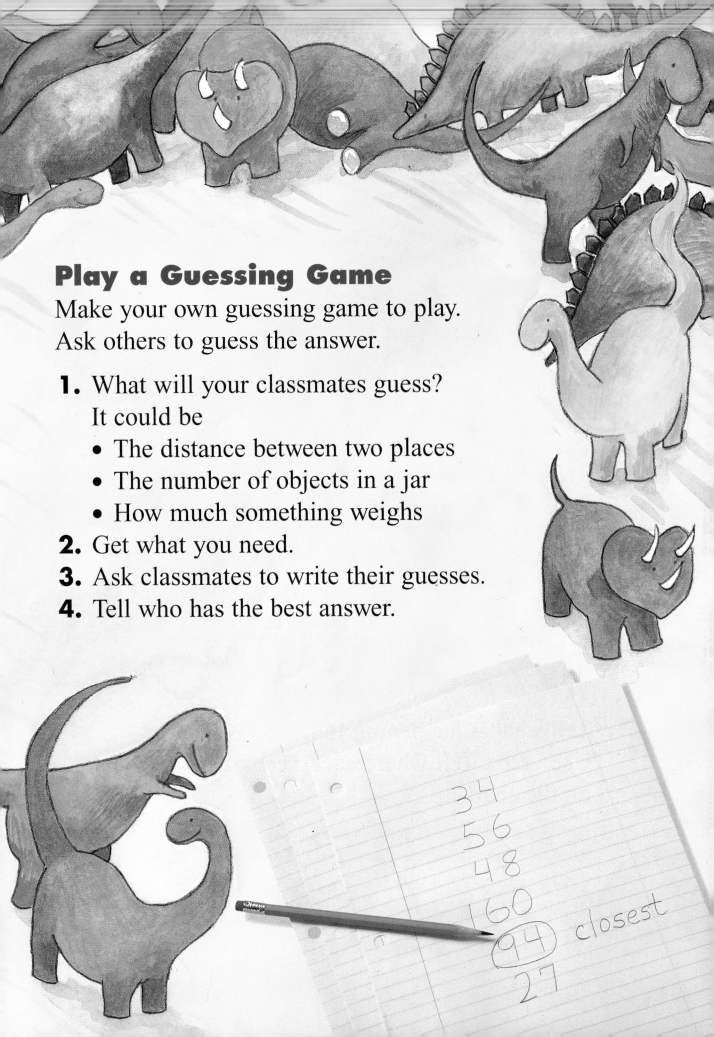

Play a Guessing Game

Make your own guessing game to play.
Ask others to guess the answer.

1. What will your classmates guess?
It could be
- The distance between two places
- The number of objects in a jar
- How much something weighs

2. Get what you need.

3. Ask classmates to write their guesses.

4. Tell who has the best answer.

34
56
48
160
(94) closest
27

Language Arts

Using Correct Verb Tenses

Every sentence has a verb. A **verb** is a word that shows action. When you write, choose the past, present, or future tense of a verb.

The children **played** a game.

The girl **plays** music.

They **will play** a new game.

past	present	future
played	plays	will play

Talk

Tell what is happening in the picture. Use verbs. Tell where each verb belongs on the chart.

Write

Write the sentences. Use a blue crayon to underline the past tense verb. Use a green crayon to underline the present tense verbs. Use a red crayon to underline the future tense verbs.

Yesterday, Mom worked hard to get everything ready for the party. Today everyone is here. Mary and Don play a game. Jane listens to music. Soon Tim will blow out the candles. We all will eat cake.

Add sentences of your own to the story. Use past, present, and future tense verbs.

A Good Laugh for Cookie

by Deborah Eaton
illustrated by
C.D. Hullinger

Buzz Gator was at it again.

Buzz loved playing jokes on his good friend Cookie.

"Hee, hee, hee," he said to himself. "This is a great one."

424

"Very funny," said Cookie.

Buzz had glued her beautiful slippers together!

Cookie would not play jokes. Sometimes she wished she could.

"Come on! Laugh!" said Buzz.

That night Cookie did not sleep well. It seemed that night would never become day. It was so dark! In fact, it was even darker than dark.

After a long time, Cookie got up and stood on her porch.

It was bright! It was sunny! Buzz had painted her windows blacker than night.

"Good afternoon!" Buzz laughed.

"Buzz Gator," said Cookie. "You could become a pest."

Later, Cookie walked in the woods.
Buzz stood behind a tree nearby.
He put on a funny mask with a hood.
"This is great!" he said. "Beautiful! Hee, hee, hee!"

Then he heard footsteps. He didn't even look. He jumped into the path and waved his arms.

"Booooo!" he yelled in his loudest voice.

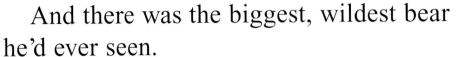

And there was the biggest, wildest bear he'd ever seen.

"Yipes! A great big bear!" Buzz cried louder than ever. Then he ran away—faster than he ever had in his life.

The next day, Buzz and Cookie were together again. "I'm sorry, Cookie. I should not have played those jokes on you," Buzz said.

"Oh, I don't mind," Cookie said.

"Maybe you'll play a good one on me someday," said Buzz. "And then we'll be even."

Cookie smiled. "Maybe I will," she said.

Moonbear's Pet

by Frank Asch

One spring day while playing in the pond Bear found
a new pet.

"Oh, what a cute little fishy!" cried his friend Little
Bird. "What will you call her?"

As Bear hurried home, he thought of names like Skinny, Sweetpea, and Slowpoke. But none of those names seemed quite right. Then he dropped his pet into a bowl of water and she landed with a *splash*. "That's it!" cried Bear. "We'll call her Splash!"

Bear and Little Bird loved to watch Splash swim and blow bubbles. They put Splash on the floor while they played and on the kitchen table while they ate.

After lunch they took Splash outside to watch while they worked in Bear's garden.

They even took Splash shopping!

Every night after Little Bird flew home to his nest, Bear stayed up late talking to Splash and telling her bedtime stories.

Every morning Little Bird brought Splash a
present: an acorn, a seashell, a pretty pebble, or
a pink button.

As the days and weeks passed

Splash grew bigger and bigger.

One day Little Bird chirped, "Look! Splash is growing wings. She must want to be a bird just like me!"

Bear took a close look at Splash. "Those aren't wings. See! There are four of them. They must be paws. Splash is becoming a bear just like me!"

"Why would anyone want to be a clumsy old bear when they could be a beautiful bird?" chirped Little Bird.

"Indeed!" exclaimed Bear. "Why would anyone want to be a chirpy sack of feathers when they could be a big strong bear?"

"Well, I guess we'll just have to let Splash decide for herself!" huffed Little Bird.

"That's just fine with me!" Bear huffed back.

So Bear and Little Bird put Splash in a tiny pool next to Bear's pond and promised each other not to visit her for a month.

"And don't visit me, either!" said Bear.

"I wouldn't dream of it!" snapped Little Bird.

Bear and Little Bird used to play together.

Now they played alone.

At the end of the month Bear and Little Bird met at Splash's pool.

"Now we'll see what a fine bear she's become," mumbled Bear.

"Or what a fine bird," grumbled Little Bird.

But Splash wasn't in the pool.

"Splash!" Little Bird called up to the sky.

"Splash!" Bear called into the woods.

Just then a young frog hopped up and croaked, "Here I am!"

"Please don't bother us now, little frog," said Bear. "We're looking for my pet, Splash!"

"But I'm Splash," said the frog.

"But you're not a bear!" said Bear.

"Or a bird!" said Little Bird.

"I was never a fish, either," said Splash. "I was a tadpole. And tadpoles don't become bears or birds. They become frogs!"

Bear was so surprised! All he could say was, "But wouldn't you rather be a bear?"

"I'd rather be a frog," said Splash.

"But wouldn't it be best if we were all birds?" said Little Bird.

"No," replied Splash calmly. "I think it would be best if we were all friends."

Bear was silent for a moment.
Then he said, "I think she's right."
"I agree," sighed Little Bird.
"I missed you, Little Bird," whispered Bear.
"I missed you too," Little Bird whispered back.
"And I missed both of you," cried Splash.
"Come on! Let's all go for a swim!"

"Good idea!" said Bear.
"Great idea!" chirped
Little Bird.
    And they all jumped
into the pond with a splash!

About the Author
Frank Asch

When Frank Asch was a child, he enjoyed nature. "I had a brook next to where I lived. I could catch frogs," he says. Mr. Asch has worked as a teacher. He has also acted with his wife in a children's theater group.

Mr. Asch loves writing for children. He believes that children bring out his "most interesting, most humorous ideas." He loves to make them laugh.

Reader Response

Let's Talk

Moonbear and Little Bird were surprised at the end of the story. Were you? Why or why not?

Let's Think

Why does Moonbear tell Little Bird not to visit him anymore?

Test Prep
Let's Write

Think of someone who is important to you. Name the person. Tell what the person looks like and what you do together.

Share Something

Think of something you care about. Tell your class about it.

1. Look at home or school. Find something you care about.
2. Think about why it is important to you.
3. Practice talking about it to a partner.
4. Show it to your classmates. Tell them about it.

Verbs: am, is, are, was, were

Some verbs do not show action. The verbs **am, is, are, was,** and **were** do not show action.

The verbs **am, is,** and **are** tell about now.

I **am** happy.

The duck **is** brown.

The frogs **are** green.

The verbs **was** and **were** tell about the past.

The dog **was** wet.

The frogs **were** in the water.

Talk

Pretend you are one of the children in the picture. Tell about yourself. Use the verbs **am, is, are, was,** and **were**.

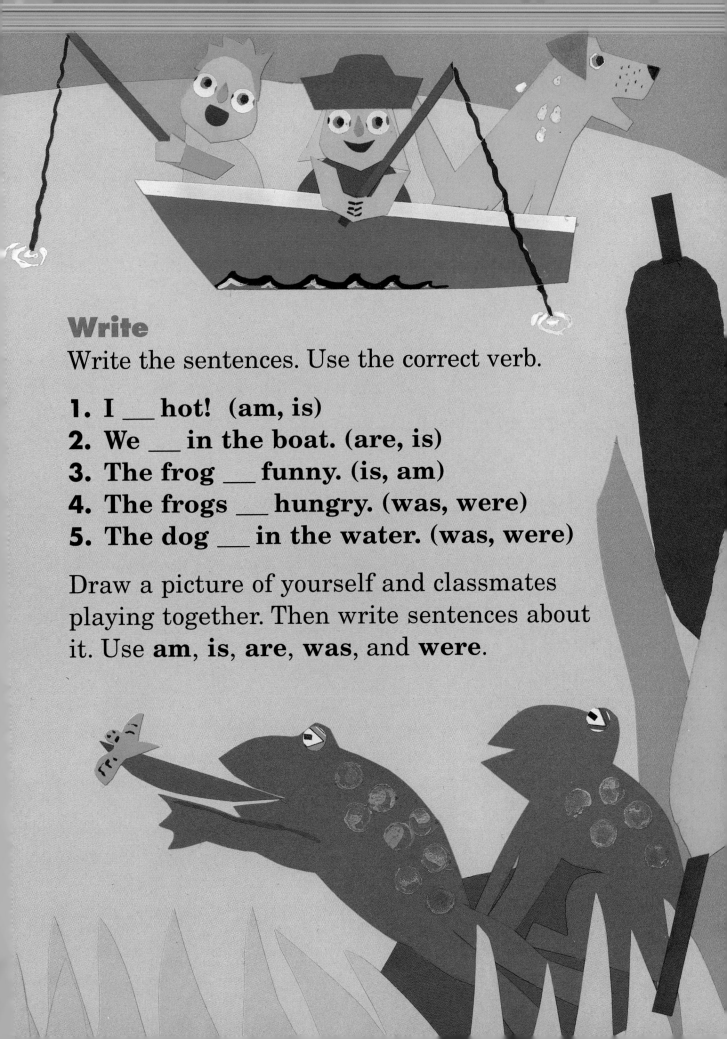

Write

Write the sentences. Use the correct verb.

1. I ___ hot! (am, is)
2. We ___ in the boat. (are, is)
3. The frog ___ funny. (is, am)
4. The frogs ___ hungry. (was, were)
5. The dog ___ in the water. (was, were)

Draw a picture of yourself and classmates playing together. Then write sentences about it. Use **am**, **is**, **are**, **was**, and **were**.

Vocabulary Review

Words I Know

How I Beat the Giants

Play Ball

baseball

pitching

returned

since

terrible

those

The Storykeeper

People, People, Everywhere!

children

city

country

dashing

high

place

room

sealing

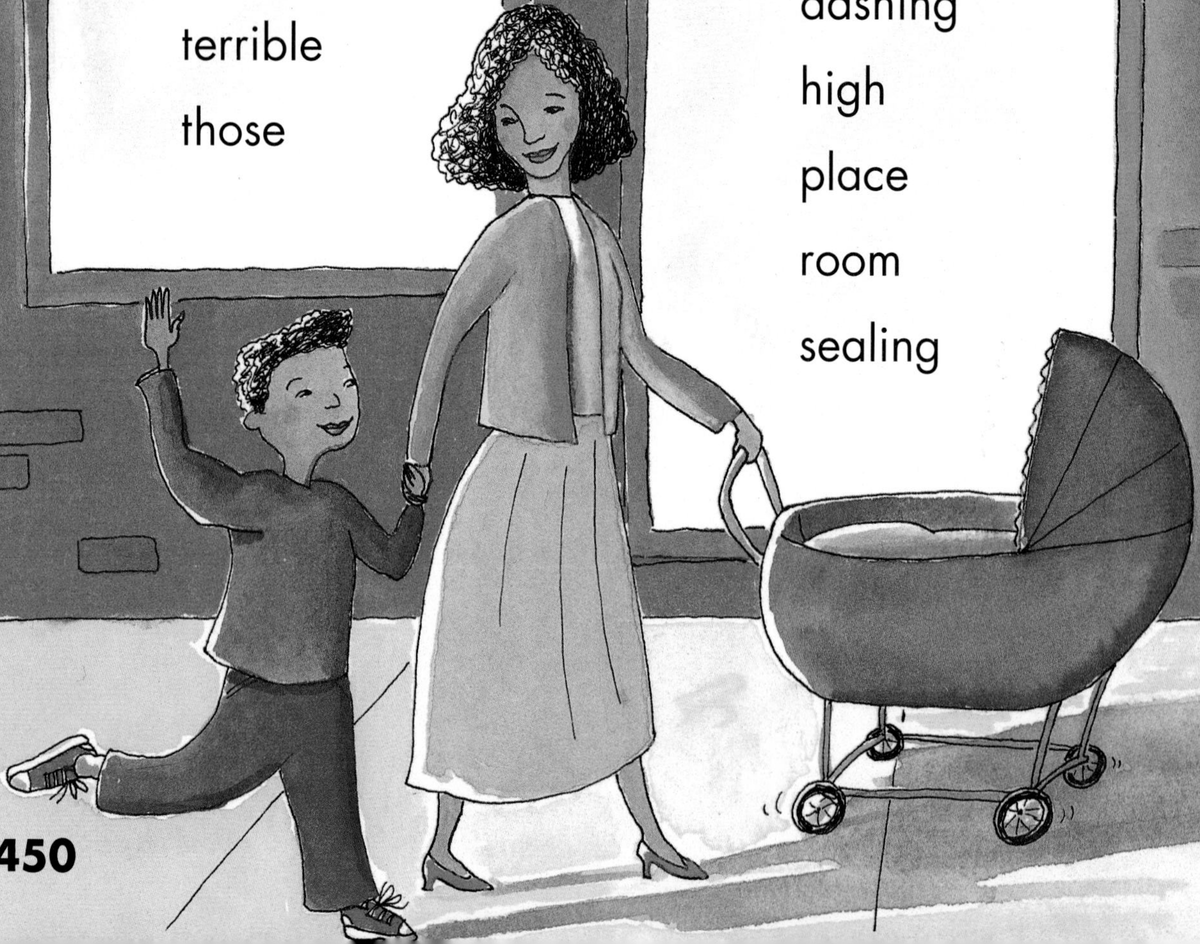

New Best Friends

WANTED:
BEST FRIEND

across

best

complained

dumped

either

sometimes

toward

Four Clues for Chee

Young
Cam Jansen

brought

camera

dinosaurs

exact

next

order

A Good Laugh for Cookie

Moonbear's
Pet

beautiful

become

bubbles

decide

paws

quite

Test Talk

Choose the Right Answer

A test may have a question and three answer choices. Only one answer is right. You must find the right answer.

A test about *Wanted: Best Friend* may have this question.

1. Why did Cat stop playing with Mouse?

Ⓐ Mouse went to the store.

Ⓑ Mouse did not want to play checkers.

Ⓒ Mouse moved away.

Read the question. What is it asking? Think about each answer choice. Choose the right answer.

Here is how one boy chose his answer.

I need to find out why Cat stopped playing with Mouse. I remember that Cat wanted to play checkers and Mouse didn't. The answer must be B.

Try it!

Use what you have learned to choose the right answer to this test question.

2. What did Cat find out after he advertised for a new best friend?

(A) Otter was fun to play with.

(B) Mole wasn't good at crazy eights.

(C) Mouse was his kind of best friend.

Glossary

Words from Your Stories

Aa

across

across

The cat is walking **across** *the street.*

another

He asked for **another** *glass of milk. The hat didn't fit, so I chose* **another.**

apartment

An **apartment** is a room or group of rooms to live in: *There are ten* **apartments** *in that building.*

Bb

baseball

baseball

1 **Baseball** is a game played with a bat and ball. Two teams of nine players each play on a field with four bases.
2 A **baseball** is also the ball used in this game.

beak

beak

beak

A **beak** is the hard part of the mouth of a bird. Another word for **beak** is **bill.**

beautiful

Beautiful means pleasing to see, hear, or feel: *We saw a* **beautiful** *swan. She had a* **beautiful** *plan.*

become

He has **become** *wiser as he has grown older. It has* **become** *warmer.*

best

Best means most excellent: *He's a good swimmer, but his brother is the* **best** *I've ever seen.* ● good, better, best.

between

There is a big rock **between** *the two trees. We'll be home* **between** *two and three o'clock.*

between

bottle

A **bottle** is something used to hold liquids. A **bottle** can be made of glass or plastic, and usually has a cap.

brain

The **brain** is the part of your body that is inside your head. You use your **brain** to learn, think, and remember. The **brain** makes it possible for you to talk, move, and see.

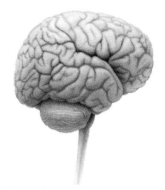

brain

brought

He **brought** *raisins in his lunch. We* **brought** *flowers for the teacher.*

bubbles

Bubbles are hollow balls of liquid floating in the air: **Bubbles** *rose up from the soapy water.*

Cc

cage

A **cage** is a box made of wires or bars: *Our pet bird sat in its* **cage.**

cage

camera

camera

A **camera** is a machine for taking pictures or making videos, movies, or TV shows.

children

Children is the plural of **child**. Young girls and boys are **children**.

city

A **city** is a large town with many people living in it. New York and Dallas are **cities**.

clean

1 **Clean** means not dirty: *I wore* **clean** *clothes.*

2 When you **clean** something, you get rid of the dirt that is in it: *We will* **clean** *the kitchen.*

climb

When you **climb**, you go up something: *Can you* **climb** *the ladder? The bikers* **climbed** *the mountain.*

climb

complained

When you have **complained**, you have said that something is wrong: *The children* **complained** *about too much homework.*

could

She **could** *ski very well. Perhaps I* **could** *go with you tomorrow.* **Could** *we go to a movie?*

country

The **country** is the land away from the city: *There were many farms in the* **country**.

Dd

dashing

dashing

Someone who is **dashing** is running very fast: *The girls are* **dashing** *to the finish line.*

decide

Decide means to make up your mind: *I* **decide** *what to wear to school.*

dinosaurs

dinosaurs

Dinosaurs were animals that lived many millions of years ago. Some **dinosaurs** were bigger than elephants. Some were smaller than cats. No **dinosaurs** are alive today.

dumped

When something is **dumped**, it is emptied out: *I* **dumped** *the books out of the bag.*

Ee

easier

When something is **easier**, it is less hard to do or understand than something else: *She thinks math is* **easier** *than spelling. Tools often make our work* **easier.**

either

Choose **either** *of these toys to give to the baby.* **Either** *come in or go out. There are lights on* **either** *side of the driveway. If you don't go, she won't go* **either.**

elephant

elephant

An **elephant** is a large, heavy animal. **Elephants** have large ears and long trunks. They use their trunks to pick up things.

enemy

An **enemy** is anything that will do harm: *The snake was the mouse's* **enemy.**

enough

Enough means as much or as many as you need: *Are there* **enough** *sandwiches for all of us? My coat is not big* **enough.**

everywhere

I looked **everywhere** *for my gloves.* **Everywhere** *we went we met people we knew.*

exact

Exact means without any mistakes: *Only one group had the* **exact** *answer.*

exclaimed

When you have **exclaimed**, you have cried out with strong feeling: *"Oh, no!" she* **exclaimed** *as she dropped her ice cream cone.*

explore

explore

Explore means to travel and to discover new places: *Astronauts* **explore** *outer space. The duckling set off to* **explore** *the pond.*

Ff

farm

To **farm** is to grow food or animals to eat or to sell: *I want to* **farm** *when I grow up.*

fix

To **fix** is to repair something that is broken: *Can you* **fix** *my watch?*

follow

Follow means to go or come after: *Let's* **follow** *him. Tuesday* **follows** *Monday.*

food

Food is anything that living things eat or drink. **Food** makes living things grow and gives them energy.

food

giggled

When you have **giggled,** you have laughed in a silly way: *The children* **giggled** *in the theater.*

guess

To **guess** is to try to give the answer to something when you are not sure: *She tried to* **guess** *before she looked up the answer. I* **guess** *it will rain tomorrow.*

Hh

have

I **have** *a nickel in my pocket. We* **have** *to go now. We always* **have** *breakfast in the kitchen. They* **have** *asked for their mail.*

hidden

Hidden means kept out of sight: *The story is about* **hidden** *treasure. The boy had* **hidden** *behind a big tree.*

hidden

high

High means up above the ground: *We walked up the* **high** *hill. The plane flew* **high** *in the sky.*

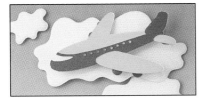

high

house

A **house** is a building where people or animals live: *She moved into a new* **house**. *I built a* **house** *for the birds.*

hundred

One **hundred** is the number after 99; 100: *There are one* **hundred** *cents in a dollar.*

Kk

keep

1 To **keep** is to have for a long time or forever: *She told me to* **keep** *the ring.*
2 To **keep** is to stay in good condition: *This coat will* **keep** *you warm.* ● **keeps, kept, keeping.**

knocked

If you have **knocked** something, you have hit it: *She* **knocked** *on their door.*

knocked

Mm

medicine

Medicine is something used to make a sick person well: *He took* **medicine** *for his cold.*

messages

1 **Messages** are information sent by one person to another: *I listened to my telephone* **messages**.
2 **Messages** are also sent from one place to another: *The eyes send* **messages** *to the brain.*

mirror

A **mirror** is a glass in which you can see yourself: *I checked my hair in the hand* **mirror**.

myself

*I can do it **myself**. I gave **myself** a haircut.*

Nn

need

If you **need** something, you are unable to do without it: *Plants **need** water to grow. I **need** new gloves for the winter.*

never

*He has **never** flown on an airplane. I will **never** get all of this work done.*

next

next

*She gave a flower to the girl **next** to her. I was sick on Monday, but returned to school the **next** day.*

Oo

order

An **order** is the way one thing comes after another in a special way: *Please line up in **order** of size to take your class picture. The words in a dictionary are in alphabetical **order**.*

outside

Outside is the opposite of inside: *The **outside** of the house needs painting. Please go **outside** and get the paper.*

Pp

paddle

paddle

Paddle means to move with the hands or feet in the water: *The duck likes to **paddle** around the pond.*

patch

A **patch** is a small piece of ground, often used to grow things: *He grows melons in the* **patch** *behind his house.*

paws

Paws are the feet of an animal that has claws. Dogs and cats have **paws.**

paws

peels

When something **peels**, the skin or covering is stripped off of it: *He* **peels** *the banana before eating it. The skin of some snakes* **peels** *off.*

pianos

Pianos are large musical instruments that you play with your fingers.

pile

A **pile** is a heap, mound, or hill of something: *The truck dumped a* **pile** *of dirt.*

pile

pitching

When you are **pitching**, you are throwing or tossing something, usually a ball: *She is* **pitching** *the ball back and forth with her sister.*

place

1 A **place** is the space where a person or thing is: *Our neighborhood is a nice* **place** *to live. Do not leave your* **place** *in line.*

2 A **place** is also a city, town, island, building, or other space: *We went to a* **place** *called Williamsburg. The auditorium is a big* **place.**

pleased

When you are **pleased**, you are happy or content with something: *He was **pleased** with his birthday presents.*

Qq _____

quiet

When something is **quiet**, it makes no sound: *It was a **quiet** night.*

quite

*There was **quite** a change in the weather yesterday. It is not **quite** five o'clock.*

Rr _____

returned

If you have **returned**, you have come back: *They **returned** from their trip early.*

ripe

ripe

When something is **ripe**, it is grown and ready to be picked and eaten: *We bought a bunch of **ripe**, yellow bananas.*

room

1 A **room** is a part of the inside of a building. Each **room** has walls of its own: *Please clean up your **room**.*

2 **Room** is also an amount of space that something takes: *There isn't enough **room** in the kitchen for everyone to sit down.*

Ss _____

scales

Scales are thin, hard pieces that form the outer covering of some fish, snakes, and lizards.

scales

sealing

If you are **sealing** something, you are closing it very tightly: *He is **sealing** the package with tape.*

should

*You **should** drink milk every day. I **should** have worn my boots.*

sick

If you are **sick**, you are feeling ill or not well: *He is **sick** and is staying in bed. I felt **sick** after riding the merry-go-round.*

sick

since

*I have been up **since** dawn. He called twice **since** Monday. **Since** you are hungry, we can have dinner now.*

sometimes

***Sometimes** my aunt takes me to the zoo. I play with them **sometimes**.*

spray

A **spray** is a liquid that flies through the air in small drops: *When the dog shook itself, we all got damp from the **spray**.*

squeeze

squeeze

To **squeeze** is to push or press hard against something: *Will you **squeeze** the oranges to make juice? **Squeeze** these books onto the shelf.*

surface

The **surface** of something is the outside part of it: *The fish came to the* **surface** *of the water. A marble has a smooth, hard* **surface.**

surprised

When you are **surprised**, you didn't know that something was going to happen: *He was* **surprised** *by her call. He* **surprised** *his friend with a present.*

surprised

Tt

taste

Taste is the flavor something has when you put it in your mouth: *The* **taste** *of sugar is sweet.*

tears

Tears are drops of salty water that come from your eyes. **Tears** fall when you cry. This meaning of **tears** rhymes with **ears.**

tears

terrible

Terrible means causing great fear: *The* **terrible** *storm destroyed many homes.*

then

The noise stopped and **then** *began again. If he broke the dish,* **then** *he should clean it up.*

those

Those *are my books.* **Those** *toys are yours, and these are mine.*

465

through

The kitten ran **through** *the house. We learned a new song all the way* **through.** *She won the prize* **through** *hard work. Dad is* **through** *working every day at three o'clock.*

thumb

thumb

The **thumb** is the short, thick finger on each of your hands.

tomorrow

Tomorrow is the day after today: **Tomorrow** *it is supposed to be rainy. We'll get together* **tomorrow.**

tools

tools

Tools are things that help you do work. Saws, hammers, rakes, and hoes are **tools.**

toward

He walked **toward** *the door.*

Uu

underneath

We sat **underneath** *the apple tree.*

until

She did not leave **until** *the following week. We waited* **until** *dark before we went in the house.*

use

When you **use** something, you put something into the action that it is meant for: **Use** *that umbrella to stay dry. We* **use** *scissors to cut paper.*

Ww

wheel

world

warm

Warm means more hot than cold: *I felt* **warm** *by the fire.*

wheel

A **wheel** is something round that turns on its center. **Wheels** help things move and work. A car has four **wheels:** *The mouse ran around a* **wheel.**

whole

1 When something is **whole**, it does not have anything missing: *I finished the* **whole** *puzzle. This is the* **whole** *class.*
2 **Whole** also means in one piece: *The dog swallowed the meat* **whole.**

world

The **world** is the Earth and everything on it.

write

When you **write**, you make letters or words with your pen, pencil, or chalk: **Write** *your name at the top of your paper.* ● **writes, wrote, written, writing.**

Writer's Handbook

Contents

Sentences

A **sentence** is a group of words that tells a complete idea.

The **subject** of a sentence tells who or what does something.
The **predicate** of a sentence tells what the subject does.

Subject	Predicate
My aunt	**plays tennis in the park.**

A **statement** is a sentence that tells something. It begins with a capital letter. It ends with a **.**.

We took a trip on our bikes**.**

A **question** is a sentence that asks something. It begins with a capital letter. It ends with a **?**.

Do you think we can get up this hill**?**

A **command** is a sentence that tells someone to do something. It begins with a capital letter. It ends with a **.**.

Get ready to clean up your desk**.**

An **exclamation** is a sentence that shows surprise or strong feelings. It begins with a capital letter. It ends with an **!**.

Terry won first prize**!**

As a writer...

I check my use of capital letters when I proofread my work.

As a writer...

I use all four kinds of sentences to tell complete ideas.

Nouns

A **noun** is a word that names a person, place, animal, or thing.

The **boy** spent his **vacation** on a **farm**.

Special names for people, places, and animals are called **proper nouns**. Proper nouns begin with capital letters.

Ms. Thomas showed us a video.

A **singular noun** names one person, place, animal, or thing.

The **frog** lives in the **pond**.

A **plural noun** names more than one person, place, animal, or thing. Add **–s** to most nouns to name more than one.

I have two **apples** in my lunch.
Sometimes I bring **pears**.

Add **–es** to a noun that ends in **s**, **ch**, **sh**, or **x** to name more than one.

How many school **buses** are there?
Mom bought **bunches** of flowers.

As a writer...

I use nouns to give my readers important information.

Some nouns change spelling
to name more than one.

Singular Nouns	Plural Nouns
goose	geese
foot	feet
tooth	teeth
wolf	wolves
leaf	leaves
mouse	mice
knife	knives

A noun that shows who or what owns something
is a **possessive noun.** Add an apostrophe **'** and **–s**
when the noun is singular.

The rabbit was a gift <u>to Sara.</u>
It is **Sara's** rabbit.

Add an apostrophe **'** after **–s** when the noun is plural.

The mother <u>of the boys</u> will be here soon.
The **boys'** mother will be here soon.

Verbs

A **verb** is a word that can show action.

The swimmer **dives** from the board.

Verbs may tell what one person, animal, or thing does. Add **–s** to these verbs.

Maddie **comes** to breakfast at 8:00.

Verbs may tell what more than one person, animal, or thing does. Do not add **–s** to these verbs.

The cars **stop** at the light.

Verbs can tell about action that takes place in the present, in the past, or in the future.

Mom **walks** the dog every day.
Mom **walked** to the store yesterday.
Mom **will walk** with me to school tomorrow.

Some verbs do not show action. The verbs **am, is, are, was,** and **were** do not show action.

Am, is, and **are** tell about now.	**Was** and **were** tell about the past.
I **am** in the second grade. Tom **is** in first grade. We **are** both in the same school.	Alice **was** in first grade last year. We **were** in the same class.

Adjectives

An **adjective** describes a noun. An adjective
may tell how many, what size, or what shape.

There are **six** presents in the bag.
They are all in **small** boxes.
They are tied with **thin** ribbons.

An **adjective** describes a noun.
An adjective may tell how
something looks, feels,
sounds, tastes, or smells.

The **yellow** rose is from Dad.
The **soft** kitten sat in my lap.
The **loud** music came from the TV.
We tried the **salty** nuts.
A **sweet** smell came from the oven.

Use adjectives when you compare nouns.
Add **–er** to an adjective when you compare
two nouns. Add **–est** when you compare
more than two nouns.

Paula is **tall**.
Tom is **taller** than Paula.
Bill is **tallest** of all.

Adverbs

An **adverb** is a word that tells about
a verb. Use an adverb to tell when,
where, or how an action takes place.

Our class will go to the museum
tomorrow. Mom and I go **there**
every Saturday. We talk **softly** in
the library.

> **As a writer...**
>
> I use adjectives to
> make word pictures
> for my readers.

> **As a writer...**
>
> I use adverbs to
> add details to my
> writing.

Pronouns

A **pronoun** is a word that takes the place of a noun or nouns. **I, he, she, it, we,** and **they** are pronouns.

Alexa rode her bicycle.
She rode her bicycle.

The day was cloudy.
It was cloudy.

Use the pronoun **I** in place of your name.

I like to play the piano.

Pronouns that tell about one person or thing are singular.

The store had many things to sell.
It had many things to sell.

Pronouns that tell about more than one person or thing are **plural**.

The computers are for our class.
They are for our class.

Singular Pronouns	Plural Pronouns
I	we
you	you
he, she, it	they

Singular Pronouns	Plural Pronouns
I	we
you	you
he, she, it	they

As a writer...

I use pronouns to take the place of nouns when the meaning is clear.

Pronouns Before and After Verbs

Some pronouns are the subject of a sentence. They come before the verb. These pronouns are **I**, **he**, **she**, **we**, **they**.

The pilot is going to Atlanta.
She is going to Atlanta.

Some pronouns come after a verb. These pronouns are **me**, **him**, **her**, **us**, **them**.

The teacher gave **Sam** a prize.
The teacher gave **him** a prize.

You can use the pronouns **you** and **it** before or after a verb.

It is on the table.
I saw **it** on the table.

Contractions

A **contraction** is a short way to put two words together.
An apostrophe ' takes the place of one or more letters.

My boots **are not** muddy.
My boots **aren't** muddy.

I will come to your house after school.
I'll come to your house after school.

Commas

Use commas to separate three or more words in a list.
I need paper, brushes, and paint for my art class.

Use a comma between the day of the week, the date, and the year.
Our hockey game is on Tuesday, May 18, 200 _.

Use a comma after the greeting and closing in a letter.
Dear Aunt Sara,

      Love,
      Trish

Sometimes two sentences are joined together by connecting words such as **and, but,** and **so**. Use a comma before the connecting word.

Tom wears gloves, and he also wears a hat.
Erin has a cat, but she also wants a dog.
My mom has a toothache, so she will go to the dentist.

Quotation Marks

Quotation marks " " show the beginning and end of what someone says.

The librarian asked, "Who would like to check out books today?"

"We would," said Juan and Angela.

Paragraphs

A **paragraph** is a group of sentences about the same idea. The first word starts a few spaces from the left. The first sentence in the paragraph often tells the main idea. The other sentences tell more about the main idea.

    Our class is putting on a play. The name of the play is *Goldilocks and the Three Bears.* One person is the narrator. Four are actors. Others are making the set and the costumes. We will invite other classes. We also will invite our families.

Writing a Thank-You Letter

A thank-you letter has the same five parts as a friendly letter. They are the **date**, **greeting**, **body**, **closing**, and **signature**. A comma goes between the date and the year. A comma is also used after the greeting and closing.

In a thank-you letter, the body of the letter thanks someone for something.

Date

October 17, 200 _

Greeting

Dear Grandma and Grandpa,

Body

Thank you for the pictures you sent. I am happy to see pictures of you when you were my age. Now, I can see why everyone in the family says I have your eyes, Grandpa, and your smile, Grandma. I have a picture of Mom when she was my age, and I can see how we all look a lot like each other. I will send you some pictures soon. Let me know who you think little brother Timmy looks like.

Closing
Signature

Love,

Kim

Addressing an Envelope

An envelope has two addresses. The **return address** tells who is sending the letter. The **mailing address** tells who will receive the letter. Use a comma between the city and state. Don't forget the zip code!

Return address

Kim Vasquez
543 Downhill Drive
Tucson, Arizona 85726

Mailing address

Mr. and Mrs. Frank Salidas
700 Franklin St.
Encino, California 91416

Sharing a Book

Writing a **book report** is one way to share a book. Here are some other ways to share.

- **Be a Reporter**
  Be a TV or radio reporter. Make a cardboard frame that looks like a TV set or a cardboard microphone for a radio report. Tell about a favorite book. You might tape-record your show.

- **Fly a Book Kite**
  Make a paper kite. Write the title and author of your book. Draw pictures about the book and write some interesting words from the book on a long paper tail. Hang the kite in your classroom.

- **Advertise on a Poster**
  Make a poster to advertise your book. Draw pictures and write some things about your book. Make your poster so interesting that your classmates will want to read your book.

- **Act It Out**
  Form a group with others who have read the same book. Make masks of the main characters.
  Take parts and act out one part or all of the book.

Spelling Lists

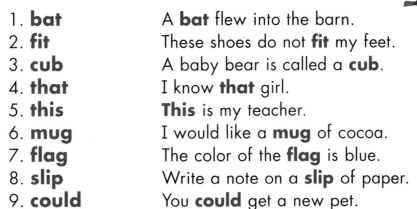

Unit 1

Franny and Ginny
Daddy, Could I Have an Elephant?

1.	**bat**	A **bat** flew into the barn.
2.	**fit**	These shoes do not **fit** my feet.
3.	**cub**	A baby bear is called a **cub**.
4.	**that**	I know **that** girl.
5.	**this**	**This** is my teacher.
6.	**mug**	I would like a **mug** of cocoa.
7.	**flag**	The color of the **flag** is blue.
8.	**slip**	Write a note on a **slip** of paper.
9.	**could**	You **could** get a new pet.
10.	**have**	I **have** three puppies.

The Wobbly People in Ellen's Block House
Poppleton and the Grapefruit

1.	**sand**	You find **sand** at the beach.
2.	**land**	Can you **land** an airplane?
3.	**send**	**Send** your mom some flowers.
4.	**desk**	Do your homework at a **desk**.
5.	**lost**	I **lost** my puppy.
6.	**last**	He was the **last** one out of the room.
7.	**pencil**	Write your name with a **pencil**.
8.	**stop**	**Stop** before you cross the street.
9.	**taste**	The **taste** of the apple is sweet.
10.	**people**	How many **people** are on the bus?

The Workers
Tools

1.	**child**	The **child** came with his mom and dad.
2.	**chin**	Dad has hair on his **chin**.
3.	**chip**	The cup has a **chip** in it.
4.	**shape**	What **shape** is a stop sign?
5.	**ship**	A **ship** sailed on the sea.
6.	**shut**	Please **shut** the window.
7.	**grade**	What **grade** are you in?
8.	**write**	I can **write** my name.
9.	**use**	**Use** a crayon to color.
10.	**world**	The **world** is round.

Spelling Lists

The Green Leaf Club News
Three Little Bikers

1. **deep**   The ocean is **deep**.
2. **seen**   Stars can be **seen** at night.
3. **free**   She gave away **free** cupcakes.
4. **leaf**   A **leaf** fell from the tree.
5. **meal**   I ate a **meal** of soup and rice.
6. **team**   Our **team** won the game.
7. **each**   We **each** had a turn.
8. **lunch**   **Lunch** was hamburgers, corn, and milk.
9. **should**   We **should** leave now.
10. **their**   He is **their** brother.

House Repair
The Surprise

1. **jumped**   I **jumped** rope with my friends.
2. **pulled**   He **pulled** the wagon.
3. **pushed**   Who **pushed** me down?
4. **crossed**   We all **crossed** at the corner.
5. **wished**   I **wished** for a new bike.
6. **picked**   Dad **picked** up the baby.
7. **candy**   **Candy** is sweet to eat.
8. **shiny**   Mom's ring is **shiny**.
9. **house**   Our **house** has five rooms.
10. **never**   I **never** ate a plum.

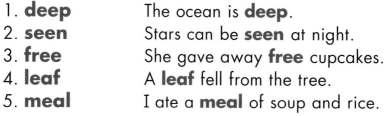

The Ugly Duckling
Unit 2 Duck

1. **passes**   Dad **passes** by my school.
2. **passing**   The clouds are **passing** by.
3. **teaches**   Mom **teaches** at school.
4. **teaching**   She is **teaching** me to sing.
5. **wishes**   I made three **wishes**.
6. **wishing**   I am **wishing** for a sunny day.
7. **danger**   The lost puppy may be in **danger**.
8. **paint**   We will **paint** the house blue.
9. **mother**   My **mother** loves me.
10. **myself**   I like **myself**.

Spelling Lists

Eye Spy
Seeing

1. **bright**   A **bright** light shined on me.
2. **sight**   The car drove out of **sight**.
3. **line**   Put a **line** under the word.
4. **side**   Whose **side** are you on?
5. **sky**   A balloon floated in the **sky**.
6. **try**   The baby will **try** to walk.
7. **hidden**   The key was **hidden** under the paper.
8. **mirror**   I see myself in the **mirror**.
9. **because**   I laughed **because** it is funny.
10. **whole**   I ate a **whole** banana.

Furry Mouse
Two Mice

1. **baby**   I have a new **baby** brother.
2. **babies**   My hamster had **babies**.
3. **bunny**   A **bunny** was in our yard.
4. **bunnies**   Four **bunnies** were in our garden.
5. **friend**   I made a new **friend** today.
6. **friends**   Mom has many **friends**.
7. **world**   Our **world** is called the Earth.
8. **dirty**   The shirt was **dirty** with mud.
9. **around**   We walked **around** in circles.
10. **food**   We need **food** to live.

The Old Gollywampus
Snakes

1. **below**   A basement is **below** a house.
2. **coat**   Put on a **coat** in cold weather.
3. **owe**   I **owe** you another dime.
4. **soap**   Wash dirty hands with **soap** and water.
5. **sold**   I **sold** my baseball cards to a friend.
6. **woke**   The baby **woke** from a long nap.
7. **everywhere**   Snowflakes fell **everywhere**.
8. **nighttime**   At **nighttime** I look at the stars.
9. **animals**   Cats and dogs are my favorite **animals**.
10. **between**   I stood **between** Mom and Dad.

483

Spelling Lists

Anansi and the Talking Melon

1.	**cage**	An animal at the zoo is kept in a **cage**.
2.	**face**	A clown's **face** is painted.
3.	**huge**	A mountain is **huge**.
4.	**page**	The **page** in the book was torn.
5.	**tease**	Don't **tease** the kitten with the string.
6.	**twice**	I fell **twice** while skating.
7.	**teachers'**	The **teachers'** coats were missing.
8.	**men's**	The **men's** laughter was loud.
9.	**until**	We stayed **until** dark.
10.	**enough**	I have had **enough** to eat.

How I Beat the Giants
Unit 3 Play Ball

1.	**hugged**	I **hugged** my mom this morning.
2.	**nodded**	Dad **nodded** his head.
3.	**skipped**	The children **skipped** along to school.
4.	**hugging**	I like **hugging** my mother.
5.	**nodding**	The girl keeps **nodding** at me.
6.	**skipping**	We were **skipping** on the playground.
7.	**crown**	The king wore a golden **crown** on his head.
8.	**shout**	Don't **shout** out the answer.
9.	**since**	It has rained **since** last night.
10.	**those**	Whose boots are **those**?

The Storykeeper
People, People Everywhere!

1.	**arm**	I fell and hurt my **arm**.
2.	**farm**	Chicks and cows live on a **farm**.
3.	**park**	We played ball in the **park**.
4.	**barn**	Hay is stored in the **barn**.
5.	**hard**	This bread is too **hard** to chew.
6.	**start**	Let's **start** the football game.
7.	**riding**	I like **riding** my bike.
8.	**moving**	My friend is **moving** away tomorrow.
9.	**city**	We live in the **city**.
10.	**place**	Take your **place** in line.

New Best Friends
Wanted: Best Friend

1. **I'll** — **I'll** come to your house later.
2. **can't** — I **can't** get the sweater over my head.
3. **he's** — I think **he's** a smart boy.
4. **I'm** — **I'm** sure my mom will not mind.
5. **didn't** — I **didn't** know the answer.
6. **she's** — **She's** the only girl on the team.
7. **spoon** — Use a **spoon** to eat cereal.
8. **through** — The thread goes **through** the hole in the needle.
9. **best** — Do your **best** on the test.
10. **sometimes** — We **sometimes** play in the snow.

Four Clues for Chee
Young Cam Jansen and the Dinosaur Game

1. **corn** — **Corn** grows tall in Mom's garden.
2. **horse** — The **horse** galloped in the pasture.
3. **pour** — **Pour** some juice in the cup.
4. **door** — Close the **door** when you come in.
5. **more** — I would like **more** bread, please.
6. **store** — Mom went to the **store** for eggs.
7. **hurries** — Dad **hurries** in from the rain.
8. **cried** — I **cried** at the end of the sad movie.
9. **brought** — I **brought** a puppet for show and tell.
10. **picture** — Dad hung up my **picture**.

A Good Laugh for Cookie
Moonbear's Pet

1. **book** — I just read a good **book**.
2. **shook** — The house **shook** in the strong wind.
3. **took** — I **took** a cookie from the jar.
4. **hood** — Does your coat have a **hood**?
5. **stood** — We **stood** in line for the movie.
6. **wood** — One pig's house was made of **wood**.
7. **bigger** — I am **bigger** than my baby brother is.
8. **littlest** — Is an ant the **littlest** insect?
9. **become** — It will **become** sunny soon.
10. **even** — The sun shines **even** in the rain.

Tested Words List

Unit 1

Franny and Ginny

Daddy, Could I Have an Elephant?
apartment
could
elephant
have
need
pianos
quiet

The Wobbly People in Ellen's Block House

"Poppleton and the Grapefruit" from Poppleton and Friends
hundred
knocked
outside
sick
taste
tears

The Workers

Tools
clean
easier
farm
fix
tools
use
world
write

The Green Leaf Club News

Three Little Bikers
climb
everywhere
giggled
should
spray
through

House Repair

"The Surprise" from Frog and Toad All Year
guess
house
never
pile
pleased
surprised
tomorrow

Unit 2

The Ugly Duckling

Duck
beak
explore
keep
myself
paddle
surface
warm

Eye Spy

"Seeing" from You Can't Smell a Flower with Your Ear
brain
hidden
messages
mirror
thumb
whole

Furry Mouse

"Two Mice" from Two Mice in Three Fables
another
bottle
cage
follow
food
wheel

The Old Gollywampus

Snakes
between
enemy
medicine
peels
scales
underneath

Spiders Up Close

Anansi and the Talking Melon
enough
exclaimed
patch
ripe
squeeze
until

Unit 3

How I Beat the Giants

"Play Ball" from Lionel and His Friends
baseball
pitching
returned
since
terrible
those

The Storykeeper

People, People, Everywhere!
children
city
country
dashing
high
place
room
sealing

New Best Friends

Wanted: Best Friend
across
best
complained
dumped
either
sometimes
toward

Four Clues for Chee

Young Cam Jansen and the Dinosaur Game
brought
camera
dinosaurs
exact
next
order

A Good Laugh for Cookie

Moonbear's Pet
beautiful
become
bubbles
decide
paws
quite

Acknowledgments

Text

Dorling Kindersley (DK) is an international publishing company specializing in the creation of high quality reference content for books, CD-ROMs, online, and video. The hallmark of DK content is its unique combination of educational value and strong visual style—this combination allows DK to deliver appealing, accesible, and engaging educational content that delights children, parents, and teachers around the world. Scott Foresman is delighted to have been able to use selected extracts of DK content within the Scott Foresman Reading program.
Page 166: *Duck (See How They Grow)* by Barrie Watts, photographer. Text copyright © 1991 by Dorling Kindersley Limited. Copyright © 1991 by Barrie Watts for photographs.

Page 12: *Franny and Ginny* © 1998 Pat Cummings.
Page 20: *Daddy, Could I Have an Elephant?* by Jake Wolf. Illustrated by Marylin Hafner. Text copyright © 1996 by Jake Wolf. Used by permission of HarperCollins Publishers.
Page 39: "Let's Play Together" from *The Magic Pocket* by Michio Mado. Copyright © 1998 by The Empress Michiko of Japan. Reprinted by permission.
Page 52: "Poppleton and the Grapefruit" from *Poppleton and Friends* by Cynthia Rylant. Illustrated by Mark Teague. Published by The Blue Sky Press, an imprint of Scholastic Inc. Text copyright © 1997 by Cynthia Rylant. Illustrations copyright © 1997 by Mark Teague. Reprinted by permission of Scholastic, Inc.
Page 76: *Tools* by Ann Morris. Text copyright © 1992 by Ann Morris. Used by permission of HarperCollins Publishers.
Page 93: "Popsicle Sticks and Glue" by Leslie D. Perkins from *School Supplies: A Book of Poems* selected by Lee Bennett Hopkins. Text copyright © 1996 by Lee Bennett Hopkins. Illustrations copyright © 1996 by Renée Flower. Reprinted by permission.
Page 104: *Three Little Bikers* by Tony Johnston. Text copyright © 1994 by Tony Johnston. Reprinted by permission of Writers House Literary Agency.
Page 127: "I Like to Ride My Bike" by Lori Marie Carlson from *Sola Sol: Bilingual Poems* by Lori Marie Carlson, illustrated by Emily Lisker. Text copyright © 1998. Illustrations copyright © 1998 by Emily Lisker. Reprinted by permission.
Page 138: "The Surprise" from *Frog and Toad All Year* by Arnold Lobel. Copyright © 1976 by Arnold Lobel. Reprinted by permission of HarperCollins Publishers.
Page 183: "Baby Chick" by Aileen Fisher from *A Frog Inside My Hat* by Fay Robinson. Copyright © 1993 by Fay Robinson. Reprinted by permission.
Page 196: "Seeing" from *You Can't Smell a Flower with Your Ear!* by Joanna Cole. Copyright © 1994 by Joanna Cole. Reprinted by permission of Grosset & Dunlap, Inc., a division of Penguin Putnam Inc.
Page 216: "Two Mice" from *Two Mice in Three Fables* written and illustrated by Lynn Reiser was originally published in *Images: Meet the Mammals* from Heath Literacy by Alvermann, et al. Copyright © 1995 by D. C. Heath & Company. Reprinted by permission of Houghton Mifflin Company. All rights reserved.
Page 225: "Mice" by Rose Fyleman from *Fifty-One New Nursery Rhymes*, copyright 1932 by Doubleday & Company, Inc. Reprinted by permission.
Page 236: *Snakes—All Aboard Reading* by Patricia Demuth. Illustrations by Judith Moffatt. Text copyright © 1993 by Patricia Demuth. Illustration copyright © 1993 by Judith Moffatt. Reprinted by permission of Grosset & Dunlap, Inc., a division of Penguin Putnam Inc.
Page 268: *Anansi and the Talking Melon* by Eric A. Kimmel & Janet Stevens. Text copyright © 1994 by Eric A. Kimmel.

Illustrations copyright © 1994 by Janet Stevens. All rights reserved. Reprinted by permission of Holiday House, Inc.
Page 312: "Play Ball" from *Lionel and His Friends* by Stephen Krensky. Illustrated by Susanna Natti. Text copyright © 1996 by Stephen Krensky. Illustration copyright © 1996 by Susanna Natti. Reprinted by permission of Dial Books for Young Readers, a division of Penguin Putnam Inc.
Page 332: *People, People, Everywhere!* by Nancy Van Laan. Illustrated by Nadine Bernard Westcott. Text copyright © 1992 by Nancy Van Laan. Illustration copyright © 1992 by Nadine Bernard Westcott. Reprinted by arrangement with Alfred A. Knopf, Inc. and Nadine Bernard Westcott.
Page 351: "City Music" © 1997 by Tony Mitton. Reprinted by permission.
Page 364: *Wanted: Best Friend* by Ann M. Monson. Illustrations by Lynn Munsinger. Text copyright © 1997 by Ann M. Monson. Illustration copyright © 1997 by Lynn Munsinger. Reprinted by permission of Dial Books for Young Readers, a division of Penguin Putnam Inc.
Page 396: *Young Cam Jansen and the Dinosaur Game* by David A. Adler, illustrated by Susanna Natti. Copyright © 1996 by David A. Adler. Illustration copyright © 1996 by Susanna Natti. Reprinted by permission of Viking Penguin, a division of Penguin Putnam Inc.
Page 419: "Sharing" from *Falling Up* by Shel Silverstein. Copyright © 1996 by Shel Silverstein. Reprinted by permission.
Page 430: From *Moonbear's Pet*, by Frank Asch. Copyright © 1997, by Frank Asch. Reprinted with permission of Simon & Schuster Books for Young Readers, Simon & Schuster Children's Publishing Division.
Selected text and images in this book are copyrighted © 2002.

Artists

John Sandford, cover, i
David Wenzel, 10
Fred Willingham, 12–19
Marylin Hafner, 20–38
Rusty Fletcher, 39
Brian Floca, 40–43
Nan Brooks, 44–51
Mark Teague, 52–64
Michele Dorenkamp, 66–69
Seymour Chwast, 70–75
David Knipfer, 76–91
Franklin Hammond, 93–97
G. Brian Karas, 4, 5, 98–131, 154–155, 456b, 481–482
Maureen Fallows, 132a
Carla Siboldi, 132–137
Janet Ocwieja, 138a, 418a
Pamela Paulsrud, 138b, 149, 160a, 236d, 268b, 312c
Arnold Lobel, 138–148
Bill Peterson, 150–153
Jacqueline Hartman, 156
Jerry Tiritilli, 6, 158–159, 483
Cheryl Kirk Noll, 160b–165
Marion Eldridge, 183
Satcey Schuett, 184–187
Chris Powers, 188–195
Neesa Becker, 196–202
C.D. Hullinger, 204–207
Lynn Reiser, 216a, 217–224
Bobbi Tull, 216c, d
John Bendall-Brunello, 225, 386–389
Shelly Dieterichs, 226–229
Mary Grand Pré, 230–235

487

Photographs

Every effort has been made to secure permission and provide appropriate credit for photographic material. The publisher deeply regrets any omission and pledges to correct, in subsequent editions, errors called to its attention.

Unless otherwise acknowledged, all photographs are the property of Scott Foresman, a division of Pearson Education. Page abbreviations are as follows: (t) top, (b) bottom, (l) left, (r) right, (ins) inset, (s) spot, (bk) background.
Page 65 (TL) © Carlo Ontal from *Best Wishes* by Cynthia Rylant, courtesy of Richard C. Owen Publishers, Inc., Katonah, NY
Page 65 (BR) Richard Hutchings for Scott Foresman
Pages 76–89 Ken Heyman/Woodfin Camp & Associates
Page 92 (TL) Courtesy Ann Morris
Page 92 (BR) Courtesy Ken Heyman
Page 118 (TL) Jack Pettee for Scott Foresman
Page 126 (CL) Courtesy Brian Karas
Page 143 Superstock, Inc.
Page 149 (TL) Courtesy, HarperCollins Publishers/Photo: Ian Anderson
Pages 166–182 © Dorling Kindersley
Page 203 (BC) Richard Hutchings for Scott Foresman
Page 216 (CL) Courtesy Lynn Reiser, Photo: Branka Whisnant
Page 224 (C) Courtesy Lynn Reiser
Page 260 (TL) PhotoDisc, Inc.; (CL) Simon D. Pollard/Photo Researchers; (CC) Larry West/Bruce Coleman Inc.; (CR) J. H. Robinson/Photo Researchers; (BG) © Orion Press/Natural Selection Stock Photography, Inc.: (CL) James P Rowan/Stone
Page 261(TL) John Serrao/Visuals Unlimited; (CL) Milton Rand/TOM STACK & ASSOCIATES; (BL) O. S. F. /Animals Animals/Earth Scenes
Page 262 (CL) James H. Carmichael/Photo Researchers; PhotoDisc, Inc.; (BR) J. H. Robinson/Photo Researchers, Inc.
Page 263 (T) Charles McRae/Visuals Unlimited; (CR) David M. Dennis/TOM STACK & ASSOCIATES; (BR) Scott Camazine/Photo Researchers, Inc.
Page 264 (TL) R. F. Ashley/Visuals Unlimited; (CR) Scott Camazine/Photo Researchers, Inc.
Page 265 (CL) Norbert Wu/Stone; (CR) Garry Walter/Visuals Unlimited; (B) Charles McRae/Visuals Unlimited
Page 266 (CL) Tom McHugh/Photo Researchers, Inc.; (BR) Bill Beatty/Visuals Unlimited: © Orion Press/Natural Selection Stock Photography, Inc.
Page 267 (TL) Larry West/Bruce Coleman Inc.; (TC) Joe McDonald/Animals Animals/Earth Scenes; (TR) Richard Walters/Visuals Unlimited; (CL) Larry Tackett/TOM STACK & ASSOCIATES; (BC) Sean Morris/O. S. F. /Animals Animals/Earth Scenes; (CR) Breck P. Kent/Animals Animals/Earth Scenes
Page 293 (TC) Eric Neurath for Scott Foresman
Page 321 (C) Frank Siteman for Scott Foresman
Page 350 Nancy Van Laan (TL) Philip Greven; (BL) Courtesy, HarperCollins Publishers
Page 385 (CL) Courtesy Lynn Munsinger; (TL) Courtesy A. M. Monson
Page 418 (TL) Courtesy David A. Adler; (BR) Courtesy Susanna Natti
Page 445 (TR) Courtesy Frank Asch
Page 457 (TL) David Young-Wolff/PhotoEdit
Page 458 PhotoDisc, Inc.
Page 461 Images reproduced from *SEE HOW THEY GROW: DUCK* with permission of DK Publishing, Inc. Dorling Kindersley
Page 467 (CL) NASA

Glossary

The contents of the glossary have been adapted from the *Scott Foresman First Dictionary*, Copyright © 2000, Scott Foresman, a division of Addison Wesley Educational Publishers, Inc.